OJIBWE
Waasa
Inaabidaa
We Look in All Directions

Gitchi-gaming onji-zaagaji-mookii
(Lake Superior from out of he emerges)

OJIBWE
Waasa Inaabidaa
We Look in All Directions

THomas Peacock
Marlene Wisuri

Foreword by Winona LaDuke

Companion to the television series by Lorraine Norrgard

Minnesota Historical Society Press

Publication of the first Afton Press edition of this book was made possible by the generous gifts and grants from:

Elmer L. and Eleanor J. Andersen
Mary A. Anderson in memory of William R. Anderson
Sarah and Beej Chaney
Alexandra and Peter Daitch
Lucy and Mark Stitzer
The Elmer L. and Eleanor J. Andersen Foundation
The Boss Foundation
The Minnesota Humanities Commission

Cover: **Circle of Life** by Ojibwe artist Joe Geshick

Created to honor our relationship with all the natural elements of the earth: the four seasons of the year, the four races of people, and the four directions, referred to in prayer as our four grandparents.

The Thunderbird, one of the most powerful creative elements from the spirit world and often a part of our ceremonies, stands in the center. The two cranes that surround the circle and connect to the roots represent our spiritual relationship with the earth. The white section of the circle symbolizes one's wholeness with God's creation — our ultimate goal, and the wavy lines are our prayers and songs to the spirit world.

Frontis: **Sunrise over Lake Superior**
photograph by Marlene Wisuri

First published 2002 by Afton Historical Society Press.

www.mhspress.org

The Minnesota Historical Society Press is a member of the Association of American University Presses.

Manufactured in Hong Kong by Pettit Network, Inc.

10 9 8 7 6 5 4 3 2 1

♾ The paper used in this publication meets the minimum requirements of the American National Standard for Information Sciences—Permanence for Printed Library Materials, ANSI Z39.48-1984.

International Standard Book Number
ISBN: 978-0-87351-785-0 (paper)

Library of Congress Cataloging-in-Publication Data
Peacock, Thomas D.
   Ojibwe waasa inaabidaa = we look in all directions / Thomas Peacock, Marlene Wisuri ; foreword by Winona LaDuke.
       p. cm.
   Originally published : Afton, MN : Afton Historical Society Press, 2002.
   Includes bibliographical references.
   ISBN 978-0-87351-785-0 (pbk. : alk. paper)
   1. Ojibwa Indians—History. 2. Ojibwa Indians—Government relations. 3. Ojibwa Indians—Social life and customs. I. Wisuri, Marlene, 1940–. II. Title. III. Title: We look in all directions.

E99.C6P446 2011
977.004'97333—dc23
                                                         2011044034

Minnesota Historical Society Press

To Bets
my partner on the path of life
who has led me back onto the good road
and caused me to dream again.

I do not wish to awaken from this dream
I do not wish to awaken from this dream
— Tom Peacock

To Jon and his people
who have enriched my life
in so many ways
— Marlene Wisuri

ACKNOWLEDGEMENTS

The work on this project would not have been possible without the support and assistance of many people, and we would like to thank them for so generously giving of their time and resources: Lorraine Norrgard and the staff and crew at WDSE Public Television for bringing us in to develop the book as an adjunct to the video series on the Ojibwe people; Lyz Jaakola for all her background and photo research; Carl Gawboy for allowing us to use his wonderful art; David Aubid for doing the translations necessary to offer photo captions in the Ojibwe language; Betsy Albert and Liz Meow for editing the manuscript; Patricia Johnston and the staff at Afton Historical Society Press for their whole-hearted support of this project. And special thanks to everyone else who helped us along the way: Wendy Savage, Phil Norrgard, Grace Grant (Baraga Historical Society), Chris Bacigalupo, Consider Burger, Patricia Lenz, Mike Cardinal, Rocky Wilkinson, Marcus Guthrie, Kathy Lyon, Dudley Edmondson, Jeff Thompson, Paul Stafford (Minnesota Office of Tourism), board of directors and staff of the Carlton County Historical Society, Dan Anderson, and our families. Special thanks to the Fond du lac Reservation, Grand Portage Reservation, and Carlton County Historical Society for their generous pre-publication purchases of the book, and to the Minnesota Humanities Commission for a publication grant. Finally, a very special thanks to our personal editors, Liz Mouw and Betsy Albert-Peacock.

Contents

Foreword

. . . Our ways are still here, our way of life. Here we are in the dying moments of the twentieth century, almost into the twenty-first-century, and we say the reality that we live within is totally different from anything we have ever known. It is just a different environment, a different context. Not a very good one, not a very harmonious or balanced one, not a very healthy one, but this is the environment that we live in today. The lifeway that spoke to our people before, that gave our people life in all the generations before us, is still the way of life that will give us life today, how it will manifest itself and find expression in this new time, comes as a part of the responsibility of how we go about the revival and renewal . . .

Jim Dumont
Fish Clan
Shawanaga First Nation

THERE IS A WORD IN ANISHINABEMO: ji-misawaabandaaming. That word, according to Earl Otchingwanigan (formerly Nyholm) describes the process as sort of positive windowshopping for your future. That is what we as Anishinaabeg need to be about. And, in order to do that, we need to recover our knowledge and recover ourselves, that is what this book is about. The story—dibaajimowin—told here is a story of Indian Country. It is the story of land-based cultures and our histories. It is also an amazing and wondrous set of stories told by those who dearly love their history and peoples—a great gift to us all: the scattered and dispersed leaves of our stories brought together with this generation's faces and living words.

Held deep within our ancestral memories, our DNA, is a magic and a beauty that is involved in this writing and in the stories. For many of us the process of recivilizing, making us conform to the dominant society—whether through boarding schools, television consumerism, or colonialism of the bodies and relatives, i.e.: land thefts, removals, and loss of biological diversity—has fragmented our psyches, our essence. Today we are in the process of remembering. And we know it is true that only through ceremony, language, feasting, dancing, and listening will we recover ourselves. The retelling of these stories nurtures that process.

In the new millennium this way of life is what we keep. We eat and cherish our wild rice, fish, deer, and plants of the woods, we live on a land that is recovering from its past abuse and whose future we hope to determine. And we work to restore ourselves to wholeness; it is ultimately our responsibility, no one else's. Anton Treuer in his book *Living Our Language* reminds us in the words of White Earth elder Joe Auginaush, "We are not losing our language, our language is losing us." Treuer takes up the battle to keep us close to our language, and he commits his soul and essence to that work, like so many of the people in *Ojibwe: We Look in All Directions*. It is that sort of courage that we need for the new millennium, the courage to be who we are.

In the meantime, the historic forces of culture-eating march forward. While we simply wish to retain and continue our lifeway, we find the global economy knocking at our door and stealing from our garden. Native peoples, not unlike indigenous species on a worldwide scale, have been isolated to islands of land within a sea of the industrial dream. Often that which is left to us and our relatives renders our cultural and biological community virtual paupers, compromised in our ability to live full and vibrant lives.

Somewhere between the teachings of Western science and those of the Native community there is some agreement about the state of the world. Ecosystems are collapsing, species are going extinct, the polar icecaps are melting, the ozone layer is withering, and nuclear radiation has contaminated the land. According to Harvard biologist Edward O. Wilson, fifty thousand species are lost every year. Three quarters of the world's birds are in decline, and one quarter of all mammals are endangered. Tropical rainforests, freshwater lakes, and coral reefs are at immediate risk, and global warming and climate change are dramatically accelerating the rate of biological deterioration.

The writing is on the wall in bold letters. In the final analysis, we humans can rationalize, revise statistical observations, extend deadlines, and make accommodations for a perceived "common good." But "Natural law" as Yakama fisherman Ted Strong explains, "is a hard and strict taskmaster." Dump dioxin into the river and you will inevitably eat or drink it. Assent to "acceptable" levels of radioactive emissions, and sooner or later those sensitive cells in the human body will likely respond.

The challenge at the cusp of the millennium is not uniquely Anishinaabeg. It is to transform human laws to match natural laws, not vice versa. In order to do that, we must close the circle. The linear nature of industrial production itself, in which labor and technology turn natural wealth into consumer products and waste, must be transformed to a cyclical system. In the best scenario, natural resources must be reused or not touched at all, and waste cut to a mere trickle.

The new era requires that we make a technological, cultural, and legal change in how we live in the larger society. Many indigenous teachings consider the present as a time of change. Anishinaabeg teachings recognize this as the time of the Seventh Fire and see this both as a reality and an opportunity. According to the prophecies of the Anishinaabeg, there are two separate paths from which to choose, for both the Anishinaabeg and the "light skinned people"—the road to technology and the road to spirituality. In the words of elder Eddie Benton Benai, a teacher of the Anishinaabeg Midewiwin Society:

[The elders] feel that the road of technology represents a continuation of head-long rush to technological development. This is the road . . . that has led to a modern society, to a damaged and seared earth. The other road represents a slower path that Traditional Native people have traveled and are now seeking again. The earth is not scorched on this trail. The grass is still growing there.

A similar teaching of the Six Nations Iroquois Confederacy tells us that "in each deliberation, we must consider the impact on the seventh generation from now."

These hopes embody that which we hope will be the future ji-misawaabandaaming—a positive future in which our land and our people are at peace. The work of our hands and our hearts and the guidance of our teachings will help us to make that positive future.

Mi'iw.

Winona LaDuke

Introduction

As a young child I spent many winter evenings sitting around the wood stove as my grandparents told stories about earlier times. There in the dim light of a gas lamp, they would weave stories about how our people survived the great forest fire that swept through the area. While many non-Indians perished, our ancestors had the sense to run to the river. They told me other stories as well, about how the people lived and how they survived and about their dreams. Maybe as a result of their teachings, I became an avid listener. And I still am.

During the preparation of this book, I was struck by the advice given to me by other Ojibwe people. Carl Gawboy, the renowned Ojibwe artist, reminded me that the book would be considered an important source of information on the Ojibwe for the next several generations, perhaps the next fifty years. Therein lies an important responsibility, he said. The next day I sat down with Marlene Wisuri and reviewed the collection of historical photographs from which but a small sample would be included in this book: a group of children waiting for a bus to take them off to boarding school; a grandmother lovingly holding her grandchild; a line of people waiting for their annuity payments. Each picture contained a whole story, few of which will ever be written. I asked myself how it came to be that I was given the enormous responsibility of helping to determine which pictures would forever represent us in history. And I went away that day greatly burdened by the responsibility suddenly thrust upon me.

I went to visit one of my brothers that evening and told him about my burden. His advice is worth sharing: "Look at their eyes and their hands. They will tell you if they should represent our story. These things are sometimes meant to be." So I have taken his advice, carefully choosing each word of narrative and working with Marlene carefully to select the pictures and artwork that will forever represent the Ojibwe in this book.

Readers will notice that I have chosen a personal story to introduce and close each chapter, and there are reasons for doing so. I refuse to distance myself from my research. My representation of the history of the Ojibwe will always contain some of my own story because I am Ojibwe. I am part of the story. These personal stories serve as a reminder to me of the indebtedness I have toward my ancestors — grandparents, great-grandparents, and the people before them, who endured and survived a horrific period of history so that I could be here today, so proud of being Ojibwe, still seeking strength in our ways, so humbled and honored to tell a part of their story.

Our ancestors spoke in quiet ways. And I am an avid listener.

— Thomas Peacock

About the photographs

The collecting, taking, and arranging of photographs for this book was akin to making a patchwork quilt. Each piece/photograph was carefully selected with an eye as to how it would contribute to the whole. As we studied the many possibilities, we weighed the relevance of each photograph to the fabric of the finished work. Tom and I deliberated over how the photographs and the text would meld to tell the story of the Lake Superior Ojibwe with facts, historical information, and a view of the natural world in a creative and beautiful way. We have tried to mirror the age-old traditions of storytelling and object making that imparted information and teaching with imagination and beauty.

When I was first approached about working on this volume, I had a number of misgivings. One of my initial hesitancies had to do with the fact that Indian people historically have been looked at through the eye of the camera (held mostly by white people) as "the other" — the people to be studied or recorded before "vanishing." I did not want to add to or perpetuate that view. In looking at so many of these wonderful old images, however, I found that even given the nature of photography's superficial recording of visible detail, there was a real sense of the spirit of the people coming through.

The Lake Superior Ojibwe had no one chronicler of the caliber of an Edward S. Curtis, who left an unforgettable, if controversial, record of many of the country's native nations. Even David F. Barry of Superior, Wisconsin, who photographed Indian people extensively in the late 1800s and early 1900s, did not often photograph his Ojibwe neighbors. Many other photographers, most of them anonymous, have left a record of the everyday life and events of the Ojibwe people. This composite image is an unromanticized view that attains beauty, not through the artistic device of a particular photographer but because of the people themselves. These people, many of them long gone from us, still have so much to teach about courage, dignity, survival, and the joy of living life to the fullest in spite of the odds.

The photographs from the 1990s were chosen to round out the whole — to add another piece to the circle of life, to present the beauty and power of the natural world, and to place the lives of the people within that world. It is our hope that this small circle will be enlarged to include many more stories and a multitude of images in an ever-widening record of the people.

As I've taken photographs and chosen images for this book, my eyes and my spirit have been refreshed by the contact with the natural world and by the images of those who have gone before us and those who are carrying on and forging new lives out of ancient traditions. For these gifts, I am grateful.

— Marlene Wisuri

The history and culture of the Ojibwe have been handed down for countless generations by the storytellers.

Story teller, acrylic on wood, Carl Gawboy

OJIBWEMOWIN
Ojibwe Oral Tradition

The Red Record: Origins, Language, and the Arts

Some time ago I was honored to attend the production of *Dear Finder*, a nationally acclaimed, locally written play that chronicles the Nazi Holocaust during the Second World War. Many who attended the play were stunned by the reminders of the profound cruelty we humans are capable of. A couple behind me were sobbing openly throughout much of the performance, as were other audience members. Even cast members' faces were wrenched with emotion when they did their final curtain call. It was a stunning, once-in-a-lifetime event that will remain forever etched in my memory, a grim reminder of the stories that must be passed down through the generations in hopes that such atrocities will never happen again.

As an American Indian who has spent a lifetime listening to and reading about the cultural obliteration and overt genocide of my indigenous ancestors, and who is confronted with the indignity of contemporary racism in all its forms on a daily basis, I was angry when I left the theater that evening. Angry because of the hypocrisy of it all. I was reminded of a time, many years ago, when, as a principal in a small reservation border school, I brought a Holocaust survivor in for an all-school program. I was confronted by parents (some of whom were members of a white supremacist group) insisting that their children not hear the speaker because, in their words, the Holocaust was "made up by the U.S. government." These same parents had made similar demands when the school added Ojibwe history to the eighth grade social studies curriculum. The same parents had proclaimed: "They don't need to learn any of that Indian stuff. Aren't we all Americans here?"

Those people, most people in fact, will never truly confront the reality of the genocide of the indigenous people of this country, the slaughter and forced death marches, or the herding of our great-grandparents, grandparents, and parents into boarding schools. Perhaps more tragically, most people will never know the beauty of our stories — the story of our creation, our migrations and history, the ways of our language, or the beauty of our art forms, which are a reflection of the Ojibwe way of being.

But mostly that evening as I watched *Dear Finder*, I was angry because just several rows in front of me were a group of Ojibwe students from a local tribal school, who already in their young lives must carry the heavy burden of racial intolerance, who like me must have realized that what happened to the Jews happened to their ancestors as well, and continues to happen to other people in the world. And I wanted to cry out to the audience: Do you see what the Nazis did to the Jews? That is also what happened to my ancestors. And I am here in front of you, and these children in front of me are here in front of you, and we are real and not part of an abstract removed past. We are not part of a play. We stand here in front of you. We want to be free and equal members of this society, and we want you to learn our story.

"We the Anishinabe people have a history that goes back 50,000 years on this continent which is now known as North America, but which has been always known to us as Turtle Island. And 50,000 years is a long, long time."
— Eddie Benton Benai

Turtle Image, watercolor, Jeff Chapman

Opposite page: The Spirit Tree near Grand Portage on Lake Superior is said to be more than three hundred years old. The site is considered sacred by many Ojibwe people.

A Chapter Road Map

BEGAMISED MIGIZI
(arrives flying he/she the bald eagle)

The soaring eagle is a powerful symbol to many Ojibwe people.

SO THE STORY BEGINS. We begin by summarizing some fundamental Ojibwe beliefs about the creation of the universe and of the earth and its re-creation following a great flood. We present several migration stories, which will show our relationship to other indigenous groups who are culturally and linguistically similar to the Ojibwe. The structure and nature of the language is discussed: its origins; its relationship to the oral tradition; the form of the written language; and the importance of language to philosophy, cultural teachings, and spirituality. We offer some insight into the influence of European colonization on language and the effects of Americanization that resulted in the loss of language. We discuss several theories of language loss and language renewal efforts in K–12 schools and colleges. We give a description of Ojibwe art: its aesthetic philosophy, medium, and music; the influences of European colonization; the efforts of contemporary Ojibwe art and artists, and its evolution. Finally, we offer a hopeful vision of the future, where Ojibwe people restore their language by implementing language maintenance and renewal programs, where non-Indians learn more about the indigenous people of this country, and where Ojibwe art thrives.

The Ojibwe Stories of Creation and Re-creation

In the story of humankind, different cultures tell parallel stories about the making of this universe in which we live and about the creation of the earth. It may never be known if these similarities are a result of a more recent melding of cultures or if the stories have a common beginning in a much larger story that has been passed down in the ancestral memory of many peoples. One example is the ancient Ojibwe story of creation, which parallels the account in the Bible's Book of Genesis.

The Ojibwe creation story is so wise, so filled with love, and so profoundly beautiful that when I first heard it, I was overcome by the deep love the Creator has for Ojibwe people. In the story, the Creator had a vision in which he saw all the things of the universe — stars and star clusters, galaxies, moons, planets, and earth. On the earth he saw oceans, lakes, rivers and streams, ponds, meadows and grasses, flowers, mountains, deserts, and forests filled with many kinds of trees and plants and animals (Johnston, 1976, p. 12):

He witnessed the birth, growth, and the end of things. At the same time he saw other things live on. Amidst change there was a constancy. Kitche Manitou [the Creator] heard songs, wailings, stories. He touched wind and rain. He felt love and hate, fear and courage, joy and sadness.

After he had envisioned these things, he brought into existence all that he had dreamed. He created the materials in which all physical things are based — wind, rocks, water, and fire — and to each he gave purpose. With these materials, he created all of the wonders of the universe — the galaxies, suns, moons, and planets, and the great voids among these worlds. Then he created the earth and all the things of the earth, and to each of these things he gave its own soul-spirit (Johnston, 1976, p. 12):

To the sun Kitche Manitou [the Creator] gave the powers of light and heat. To the earth he gave growth and healing; to waters purity and renewal; to the wind music and the breath of life itself.

On earth Kitche Manitou formed mountains, valleys, plains, islands, lakes, bays, and rivers. Everything was in its place; everything was beautiful.

NINGIJIWANANSING
(melting running water place)

He then created plants and put them in places on the earth where they would be the most useful to other plants, animals, and people, and he gave each of them a purpose and reason for being —

growing, healing, and beauty. Next to be created were our elder brothers, the animals — the fishes, four-leggeds, birds, and those that walk on two legs. Each of our elder brothers was given a special reason for being, special power, and his own unique way.

Last in the order of creation were people and the great natural laws that govern all life on this earth (Johnston, 1976, p. 13):

Though last in the order of creation, least in the order of dependence, and weakest in bodily powers, man had the greatest gift — the power to dream.

Kitche Manitou then made the Great Laws of Nature for the well being and harmony of all things and all creatures. The Great Laws governed the place and movement of sun, moon, earth and stars; governed the powers of wind, water, fire, and rock; governed the rhythm and continuity of life, birth, growth, and decay. All things lived and worked by these laws.

Kitche Manitou had brought into existence his vision.

Like the accounts of many cultures of this earth, Ojibwe stories tell of a great flood and of the re-creation of the earth following the flood. This is the story of Turtle Island, told in other versions among many of our Ojibwe relatives. A great flood had befallen the earth, consuming with it all animals and plants and leaving only the fishes, birds, and animals that lived in water. A spirit woman living in the heavens was having great trouble, and the animals pitied her and asked a giant turtle to rise out of the water so the woman could come to rest on its back. Once there, she asked the animals to get some earth from the bottom of the sea. The beaver, fisher, marten, and loon all tried but to no avail. Finally, the muskrat tried; his attempt was at first greeted with scorn from the rest of the animals. After a long time, however, he emerged from the depths of the waters with a small piece of earth in his paws. Johnston (1976) describes the rest of the story (p. 14):

While the muskrat was tended and restored to health, the spirit woman painted the rim of the turtle's back with the small amount of soil that had been brought back to her. She breathed upon it and into it the breath of life. Immediately, the soil grew, covered the turtle's back, and formed an island. The island formed in this way was called Mishee Mackinakong, the place of the Great Turtle's back, now known as Michilimackinac. The island home grew in size. As the waters subsided, the animals brought grasses, flowers, trees, and

> "Our history tells us that long, long ago there was a flood."
> — Eddie Benton Benai

MOOZOOG
(moose)

And next to be created were our elder brothers the animals — the fishes, four-leggeds, birds, and those that walk on two legs.

food-bearing plants to the sky-woman. Into each she infused her life-giving breath and they lived once more. In the same way were the animals who had drowned revived. Everything was restored on that island home.

These great stories of the creation and re-creation were passed down to us through the generations in the ceremonies, prayers, and songs that are so much a part of Ojibwe culture.

Muskrat. While resting on the back of a giant turtle, the spirit woman asked the animals to get some earth from the bottom of the sea. The beaver, fisher, marten, and loon all tried to no avail. Finally, the muskrat tried. After a long time, he emerged from the depths of the waters with a small piece of earth in his paw.

The migration routes and areas of settlement of the Ojibwe in the Lake Superior region

Migrations of the Ojibwe

There is some comfort in believing we have always been in the places that we now call home. We know, however, that the Ojibwe communities in which we live, be they Odana, Lanse, Red Cliff, White Earth, or Turtle Mountain, are all relatively new in the long story of our people. Many of the stories that explain our migrations to these contemporary places remind us that we may have been here once before, in a time now hidden somewhere in our ancestral memory. We do know that much of contemporary Ojibwe country was covered with a sheet of ice several miles thick nearly twelve thousand years ago during the last glacial period. With the retreat of the ice came the return of plants — trees and grasses and flowers. Then our elder brothers, the four-leggeds and birds, called this home. Then the people of other nations called this home, the Cheyenne, Blackfeet, Dakota, Fox, and Menominee.

The ancestors of the Ojibwe were the Lenni Lenape (known today as the Delaware), the Grandfathers, who migrated across this great continent from the west to the east (Peacock, 1998):

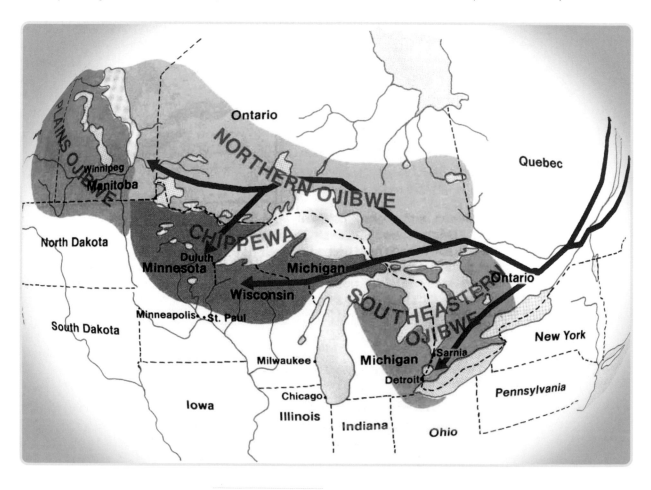

MICHILIMACKINAC
(place of the Great Turtle's back)

Mackinac Island, fort, and trading community. Round Island, just off the harbor, was used for Ojibwe encampments. The Ojibwe lost this area to the British in 1781.

The Lenni Lenape are the original people from which many tribal nations, including the Anishinabe, trace their ancestry. The story of this period of our migration is what connects us as cousins to western and midwestern tribes — Blackfeet, Cheyenne, Cree, Shawnee, and Miami to name a few. Next was the journey north and that connects us as relatives to the eastern nations — including the Passamaquaddy, Penobscot, and Wampanoag. More recently our ancestors began a westward migration as one people with the Ottawa and Potawatomi only to split and become separate nations along the way. This journey eventually led us to Madeline Island (just offshore Red Cliff, Wisconsin).

The Red Record

An epic story of migration, known as the Wallum Olum, was told by our ancient ancestors, the Lenni Lenape. Recorded on bark tablets and song sticks, this written record is the oldest recorded account of people in North America, dating back before 1600 b.c. (McCutchen, 1993):

Among Native Americans — whose elders are given respect and for whom a title of age is proof of honor and influence — the Lenni Lenape were known as the "Grandfathers"; they were acknowledged as the progenitor tribe of what the French called the grand old Algonquian Family.

Few contemporary Ojibwe really know the story of the Wallum Olum because we have chosen to concentrate on our most recent migration from the area that is now Newfoundland. But the Red Record tells of a time long before that, and it is a story that needs to be told again (Peacock, 1998):

The Wallum Olum describes a journey from the west to the Atlantic Ocean, of the eventual dispersion of the people as they branched out and became their own nations, took on new names, and evolved into the tribes we know today. The journey has our ancestors as far west as California, the home of our Lenape relatives, the Yuroks and Wiyots. Amelia LeGarde, a highly respected Ojibwe storyteller, noted that at one time our people were in the west, "as far as California." The Wallum Olum tells of the encounters as they journeyed east and

The fur trade had a tremendous effect on Ojibwe life and culture. This painting depicts the return of a voyageur to his family in Grand Portage.

came upon the indigenous people of the Rockies and Great Plains, the great mound builders of the Mississippi, and eventually with our traditional enemies, the Iroquois. Other tribes with Lenape roots, including the Cheyenne, Arapaho, Cree, Blackfeet, Shawnee, and Miami may have settled as others made their eastward journey, or like the Ojibwe moved east only to move westward in another migration. Eventually, the Lenni Lenape reached the Atlantic Ocean and settled along the Delaware River. From there, some of them branched out to the north to New England, to become our relatives, the Montauk, Wampanoag, Pequot, Narraganset, Nipmuc, Penobscot, Passamaquaddy, and others. Others, including the Ojibwe, moved north to the St. Lawrence River area in what is now Newfoundland, and then west. The last entry of the Wallum Olum was written in 1638 to announce the arrival of a boat load of European settlers. The statement is both chilling and prophetic, saying simply, "Who are they?"

Ojibwe canoers at Sault Ste. Marie, which was historically important to the Ojibwe

Village at Sault Ste. Marie

The Ojibwe migration from the area now known as Newfoundland
Our ancient ancestors lived on and near the Atlantic Ocean nearly six hundred years ago near the mouth of the St. Lawrence River (Warren, 1974). Johnston (1976) indicated that they lived there for so long that most forgot their true origins lay in the west. The westward migration began as a journey as one people with the Ottawa (Odawa, or traders) and Potawatomi (keepers of the perpetual fire). Separation of the three peoples came at the Straits of Michilimacinac (where Lake Michigan converges with Lake Huron). At that point, some Ojibwe proceeded north and became the first nation Ojibwe of Canada and the ancestors of the people of present-day Grand Portage in Minnesota and Turtle Mountain in North Dakota. Another group went south and west to the areas where we live today. The Ottawa chose to stay near Sault Ste. Marie and the Pottawatomi moved into northern Michigan. This second migration was described by Warren (1974, p. 78-79) as he heard it at a Midewiwin ceremony. He was told:

While our forefathers were living on the great salt water toward the rising sun, the great Megis (sea-shell) showed itself above the surface of the great water, and the rays of the sun for a long period were reflected from its glossy back. It gave warmth and light to the Anishinabeg. All at once it sank into the deep, and for a long time our ancestors were not blessed by its light. It rose to the surface and appeared again on the great river which drains the waters of the Great Lakes, and again for a long time it gave life to our forefathers, and reflected back the rays of the sun. Again it disappeared from sight and it rose not, till it appeared to the eyes of the Anishinabeg on the shores of the first great lake. Again it sank

Moningwunakauning
(place of the golden-breasted woodpecker)

La Pointe, or Madeline Island, the great homeland of the Ojibwe people

from sight, and death daily visited the wigwams of our forefathers, till it showed its back, and reflected the rays of the sun once more at Boweting [Sault Ste. Marie]. Here it remained for a long time, but once more, and for the last time, it disappeared, and the Anishinabeg was left in darkness and misery, till it floated and once more showed its bright back at Moningwunakauning [Madeline Island in Lake Superior], where it has ever since reflected back the rays of the sun, and blessed our ancestors with life, light and wisdom. Its rays reach the remotest village of the widespread Ojibways.

An interpretation was then offered to Warren (p. 79-80):

My grandson, said he, the megis I spoke of, means the Me-da-we [midewiwin] religion. Our forefathers, many string of lives ago, lived on the shores of the Great Salt Water in the east. Here it was, that while congregated in a great town, and while they were suffering the ravages of sickness and death, the Great Spirit, at the intercession of Manabosho, the great common uncle of the Anishinabeg, granted them this rite wherewith life is restored and prolonged. Our forefathers moved from the shores of the great water, and proceeded westward. The Me-da-we lodge was pulled down and it was not again erected, till our forefathers again took a stand on the shores of the great river where Mon-ne-aung (Montreal) now stands.

In the course of time this town was again deserted, and our fore-fathers still proceeding westward, lit not their fires till they reached the shores of Lake Huron, where again the rites of the Me-da-we were practiced.

Again these rites were forgotten, and the Me-da-we lodge was not built till the Ojibways found themselves congregated at Boweting (outlet of Lake Superior) where it remained for many winters. Still the Ojibways moved westward, and for the last time, the Ma-da-we lodge was erected on the Island of LaPointe

[Madeline Island], and here, long before the pale face appeared among them, it was practiced in its purest and most original form.

Madeline Island, which lies so majestically just offshore from Red Cliff, Wisconsin, is the great homeland of the Ojibwe. Most of our Ojibwe ancestors originally came from Madeline Island. There they lived in a large community estimated at over ten thousand people (Warren, 1974, p. 96-97):

For greater security they were obliged to move their camp to the adjacent island of Moningwunakauning (place of the golden-breasted woodpecker, but known as LaPointe). Here, they chose the site of their ancient town, and it covered a space about three miles long and two broad, comprising the western end of the island.

While hemmed in on this island by their enemies, the Ojibways lived mainly by fishing. They also practiced the art of agriculture to an extent not since known amongst them. Their gardens are said to have been extensive, and they raised large quantities of Mundamin (Indian corn) and pumpkins.

The more hardy and adventurous hunted on the lake shore opposite their village, which was overrun with moose, bear, elk and deer. The buffalo, also, are said in those days to have ranged within a day's march from the lake shore, on the barrens stretching towards the headwaters of the St. Croix River.

Bear Feast at Lac Courte Oreilles, 1941. Sharing, feasting, and the coming together of the generations were important activities among Ojibwe people.

The Ojibwe lived on Madeline Island for 120 years before it was suddenly abandoned. Warren felt the coming of Europeans, the advent of the fur trade, and the subsequent introduction of the firearm led to a rapid expansion of the Ojibwe into Wisconsin and Minnesota, where they were able to overpower the Fox and woodland Dakota easily with their superior weaponry. Warren also told of a period of starvation and disease on the island as the main cause for its abandonment.

The Ways of the Language

The linguistic origins of the Ojibwe language (ojibwemowin or anishin-abemowin) are linked to a larger language and cultural group often misnamed the "Algonquian" or "Algonkin". The common origin of all Lenape people also defines the linguistic relationship with our close relatives, including the Mohicans, Nanticokes, Shawnee, Cheyenne, Penobscots, Passamaquaddy, Wampanoag, Odawa, Potawatomi, Mesquakie, and others. John Nichols, an expert in the language, noted that (Vizenor, 1984, p. 16):

Ojibwe and the other languages grouped together in the Algonquian family resemble each other so closely in sound patterns, grammar, and vocabulary that at one time they must have been a single language; as the speakers of this ancient language, no longer spoken, became separated from one another, the way they spoke changed in different ways until we have the distinct languages spoken today. . . . At the time of the European invasion of North America, the languages of the Algonquian language family were spoken by Indians along the Atlantic coast from what is now North Carolina to Newfoundland, inland across Canada to the Great Plains, and in the region of the Great Lakes, perhaps ranging as far south as Alabama and Georgia.

Tradition bearer Nick Hocking of Lac du Flambeau passing on his knowledge of Ojibwe ways at Fond du Lac Tribal and Community College

The Oral Tradition

The Ojibwe are a story people, and stories have been the most common means by which the history and culture have been passed down through the generations. While there is much depth, subtlety, and nuance in many of these stories, there are also simple and universal teach-ings. Children as well as adults find meaning in these stories. In traditional times, stories were the way in which the world was explained to Ojibwe children, with a great variety of stories revolving around many themes, including "hunger, courage, generosity, fidelity, creation, death, the nature and essence of being, the tone of life, the quality of existence, transformation, history, and all matters of mankind" (Johnston, 1976, p. 123).

Of all the Ojibwe stories, those told of Waynabozho (also called Nanabozaho, Manabozo, Nanabush, or Naanabozho), the great teacher of the Ojibwe as well as the trickster, are the most widely known throughout Ojibwe country. Waynabozho stories are used to explain the why and how of many things — why white birch trees have black marks on them, why hell divers walk the way they do, how the new earth was created after the great flood, and so on.

Through the ages our stories have grown and changed to fit the times. That is the nature of stories. Clifford (1986, p. 100) said, "Any story has a propensity to generate another story in the mind of the reader (or hearer), to repeat and displace some prior story." Stories, many rich in metaphor, remain the way in which knowledge, and ultimately wisdom, is passed down in Ojibwe communities (Copway, 1987, p. 72-73):

The winter season was a time for storytelling, making and repairing things, and trapping. It was a harsh time for the People.

The Ojibways have a great number of legends, stories and historical tales, the relating and hearing of which form a vast fund of winter evening instruction and amusement.

There is not a lake or mountain that has not connected with it some story of delight or wonder, and nearly every beast and bird is the subject of the story-teller, being said to have transformed itself at some prior time into some mysterious formation — of men going to live in the stars, and of imaginary beings in the air, whose rushing passage roars in the distant whirlwinds.

These legends have an important bearing on the character of the children of our nation. The fire-blaze is endeared to them in after years by a thousand happy recollections.

Written Language

An enduring misconception among many Euro-Americans is that the indigenous people of this continent were illiterate, relying solely on oral stories to pass down the history and culture of their nations. Many tribes, however, including the Ojibwe, possessed complex, highly compressed forms of written language. Another debate raging among theorists and researchers in academic communities has been whether there are substantial differences between the thinking of people from oral traditions versus literate ones. Silvia Scribner and Michael Cole (1981) found that differences in thinking are more a function of schooling than of literacy. J. Peter Denny (1991) reported that all humans use rationality, logic, generalizing abstraction, insubstantial abstraction, theorizing, intentionality, causal thinking, classification, explanation, and originality. Denny summarized the research: "Cross-cultural differences in thought concern habits of thinking, not capacities for thought. . . . Different cultures make some of these thought patterns fluent and automatic, whereas the opposite patterns remain unusual and cumbersome" (1991, p. 66).

The one difference that most current theorists and researchers recognize between oral and literate people is the contextualized

Fish Dance at Lac du Flambeau

Marcella La Pointe, then a first grader at the Fond du Lac Ojibwe School, learning the Ojibwe language, 1990

"No longer would they think Indian or feel Indian [if the Indian people lost the Ojibway language]."

— Basil Johnston

thought of people from oral traditions and the decontextualized thought of those from literate traditions (though researchers hold that literacy is not the sole cause of decontextualized thought). The ability to write to distant audiences, what British writer Margaret Donaldson (1979) called "disembodied" thought, what some Americans called "elaborated" thought, and what Australians and current American oralcy/literacy theorists call "decontextualized" thought, is one characteristic that separates oral from literate discourse communities. This may explain both the difficulty of communicating concepts of the Ojibwe way of being in written English and the difficulty some young Ojibwe have with writing the English language.

In the Wallum Olum, there is a depth of meaning to each word, which is not often found in language today (McCutchen, 1989, p. 15):

The language and form of the Red Record [Wallum Olum] are distinctive. Its 687 words are the lyrics of a song, cryptic, poetic, highly compressed. It is in an archaic form of the language, like the English of Shakespeare or the King James Bible. One reason the Red Record has been so difficult to translate until now is the density of meaning packed into each of its carefully chosen words.

Our Ojibwe ancestors also used a form of this written language to record history and spiritual teachings on rocks, song sticks, birch bark, wood, wampum strings, and belts (sometimes made with sea shells). Copway noted how these written records were preserved and passed down through the generations (McCutchen, 1989, p. 33-34):

There is a place where the sacred records are deposited in the Indian country. These records are made on one side of bark and board plates, and are examined once [every] fifteen years, at which time the decaying ones are replaced by new plates. . . . The guardians had for a long time selected a most unsuspected spot, where they dug fifteen feet, and sank large cedar trees around the excavation. In the center was placed a large hollow cedar log, besmeared at one end with gum. The open end is uppermost, and in it are placed the records, after being enveloped in the down of geese or swans.

The Relationship of Language to Ojibwe Lifeways

Copway's description of the secret storage shelters for the sacred scrolls highlights the close relationship of the philosophy, cultural teachings, and spirituality of the Ojibwe to the language in both its written and oral forms. There are several schools of thought on the links between language and culture. One belief holds that language contains all the subtleties, nuances, and deeper meanings of culture and that without language a culture will die (Reyhner, 1996, p. 4):

Languages contain generations of wisdom, going back into antiquity. Our languages contain a significant part of the world's knowledge and wisdom. When a language is lost, much of the knowledge that language represents is also gone. Our words, our ways of saying things are different ways of being, thinking, seeing, and acting.

Another school of thought holds that vestiges of culture exist regardless of language. Cultural mannerisms (many Ojibwe people, for example, point with their lips), cultural events (the contemporary pow-wow), and means of survival (harvesting wild rice and making maple sugar) are ways of transmitting cultural knowledge and history through English rather than Ojibwe language.

Whether one agrees or disagrees with arguments on the relationship of culture to language, the fact remains that our spiritual teachings and ceremonies are all done in the Ojibwe language. Without knowledge of the language, listeners do not know the meanings of stories, prayers, or songs. Language and culture, therefore, are intricately interwoven.

Ojibwe Contact with Europeans

Warren tells the story of the Ojibwe people's knowledge of the coming of Europeans (1984, p. 17): "The Ojibways affirm that long before they became aware of the white man's presence on the continent, their coming was prophesied by one of their old men, whose great sanctity and oft-repeated fasts enabled him to commune with spirits and see far in the future." He goes on to say that the Ojibwe knew they would be removed from their lands and

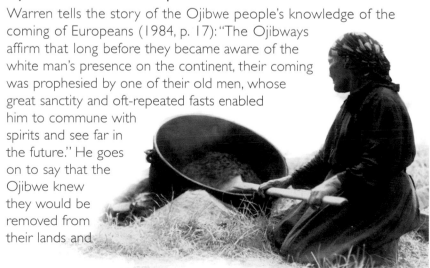

that the coming of the whites would eventually lead to the end of the world. Warren also gives an account of the first encounter with Europeans. Ma-se-wa-pe-ga (Whole Ribs), an Ojibwe spiritual leader living on Madeline Island, dreamed of the coming of the white race to the East Coast. Once he had gathered enough provisions for travel, he made the journey east with his wife and encountered the Europeans for the first time. Upon returning to Madeline Island with presents of a steel ax, knife, beads, and a piece of cloth, he shared the tale of his journey with the men of the tribe. The following year, a large group set out from Madeline Island with furs for trading and returned with their first firearms and alcohol.

Written records of Indian-white contact have been kept primarily by non-Indians in Jesuit missionary journals, fur trade journals, personal correspondence, church records, and governmental documents. While these records capture only one part of the story, these accounts nonetheless provide great insight into the intercourse between the two peoples and the effects of European colonization on the Ojibwe.

Partially as a result of the great friendship that developed between the Ojibwe and the French and the resulting intermarriage (many of these mixed-bloods became traders, also called the Voyageurs), the Ojibwe language became the language of the fur trade in the Great Lakes region and was even used in the exchanges between the French and other tribes. There were, however, other instances when the Ojibwe language was used for purposes of assimilation. Accompanying the French traders were missionaries, who had long developed a system of converting indigenous people to Christianity by first learning and then translating the languages into hymns as well the Christian Bible. Father Frederic Baraga wrote the first Ojibwe language book.

The assimilation of the indigenous peoples of this continent continued during the period of American colonization. A major external force leading to the decline of the Ojibwe language was when Ojibwe children were sent to mission schools and later boarding schools, where speaking Ojibwe was strictly forbidden. Grover's (1999) description of Ojibwe people in boarding schools offers riveting, heart-wrenching stories about the schools' effects on language and culture. At the same time, the practice of the Ojibwe spiritual ceremonies (Ojibwe language and spiritual practices are intricately interwoven) was banned by government agents.

Internal influences — such as moving off the reservation, getting a job (where English was often required), listening to media (radio and television), and the attraction to mainstream culture — have contributed to language loss. A changing value system in some Ojibwe communities, where language was not seen as important, continued the decline. Furthermore, many efforts at renewal have focused more on language appreciation, learning all the basic words and phrases rather than teaching for fluency, which has had little impact on the decline in language usage. Rosemary Christensen, a Mole Lake Ojibwe, conducted a study of Ojibwe language usage in the three-state area of Michigan, Wisconsin, and Minnesota. Her study (Christensen, Ruhnke, and Shannon, 1995) found fewer than five hundred fluent Ojibwe speakers in the three-state area, with none under the age of forty-five. Many were elders. They found no children who were fluent in the language.

Father Frederic Baraga, known as the "snowshoe priest," was a missionary among the Ojibwe of the Lake Superior region. Baraga developed a dictionary of the Ojibwe language.

Ojibwe children and James A. McFarland, teacher, standing in front of Grand Portage School, 1889. Speaking the Ojibwe language was strictly forbidden in early schools.

How do we know when a language is in trouble? One such definition was offered by Crawford (1996), who outlined the tell-tale signs of a language in trouble: a decline in the number of speakers; fluency increases with age; use decreases in social gatherings, ceremonies, cultural observances, and in the home; and parents fail to teach their children the language. Many Ojibwe communities are left with a handful of fluent speakers, and the language is rarely heard except in some tribal school classrooms, tribal college classes, ceremonies, and feasts. Ojibwe is seldom the language of everyday social discourse, and English is the language of government and commerce in many Ojibwe communities. If we consider Crawford's description of language loss and apply it to our own communities, we will have a better insight into the extent of language loss.

What are the effects of language loss? History holds countless stories of the extinction of languages and cultures. My own fear of the language crisis echoes that of other Ojibwe people (Cleary and Peacock, 1998, p. 123-124):

My children have also taken Ojibwe language classes. The oldest (Brady) has taken courses in the language up to level six (whatever that is). The youngest (Beau) has practiced his budding language skills at the dinner table, asking me to pass the butter (dodoshabo bimiday), milk (dodoshabo), or bread (bakwayzhegun). But it always leaves me wondering what will remain of a language that was spoken by our ancestors for countless thousands of years. Like Latin, will it be relegated to academia, to be taught and spoken only in area tribal schools and universities? Will it only survive in sparsely distributed Ojibwe coloring books? Will it survive in our ceremonials only until the last elder has passed on? Will it survive only in church hymns or in fractured sentences around dinner tables? These are troubling questions in need of serious discussions and decisions.

Cultures and languages are like living organisms in that they change and adapt with time and circumstances. Because of this, linguists often put the life span of a language at twelve thousand years. This evolution results from changes in culture, a culture's intercourse with people from other cultures, and with the need for descriptions of new things, animals, people, and encounters. Some examples of this in the Ojibwe language are words like *ba-ka-a-quay*, or chicken, a relatively new word. *Boozho* (hello), a word adopted from the French, and o-da-ban (car), which sounds similar to the German word for highway (autobahn). So it may be that the Ojibwe language is evolving to fit the times and will survive despite the odds.

In some respects, we have a great deal to say about whether the language survives. Recent efforts to teach the language to young people — as seen in both public and tribal schools throughout Ojibwe country and in local tribal, state, and private colleges and universities — hold out some hope. Immersion programs are becoming more common in some communities. The Mille Lacs Band of Ojibwe, for example, teaches language using music. The University of Minnesota-Duluth hosts an annual Ojibwe language immersion camp. Fond du Lac Tribal and Community College has put the language on the internet, where it is accessible to anyone who is linked to the World Wide Web. Leech Lake Tribal College has a strong focus on language preservation. Bemidji State University (Minnesota) publishes a regular journal on the Ojibwe language. More recently, Ojibwe people from all over gathered on the Mille Lacs Reservation to discuss issues of language restoration. This historic gathering of spiritual people, teachers, and other leaders may well put us on the pathway to language restoration and maintenance. Ojibwe people seem to be increasingly aware of the language crisis, and more determined than ever to take steps to ensure the language of our ancestors is spoken far into the future.

What will assure the language will survive? While the future is impossible to predict, it may be that the Ojibwe spoken by our elders will survive through technology, such as videotapes, tape recordings, CD-ROM, DVD audio, and other formats yet to be developed. With the help of technology, the spoken word will be preserved indefinitely and, like Hebrew, may be revived to be spoken again by our grandchildren and their children.

A Description of Ojibwe Art Within the Context of Tradition

I have been well educated in the history, literature, and art of the European colonizers. One result of this is a real appreciation for European art. I have been fortunate to have traveled to Paris on several occasions, where I have taken walking tours of that old and beautiful city of light, full of intricate stone architecture and wonderful museums. In that ancient and profoundly beautiful city, I have spent much time walking along the Left Bank of the Seine River, an area known in part for its numerous street artisans who will create your portrait for a hundred francs or more. In the Cathedral of Notre Dame, I listened to the haunting music of the Gregorian chants. My life partner and I have spent hours in the Louvre, which houses the works of the great European masters, including Da Vinci's *Mona Lisa*. A short walk across a bridge over the Seine is the Musée d'Orsay, one of my favorite museums because it

Pictography was used in both secular and sacred contexts among the Ojibwe people.

Woman with Blueberries,
watercolor by Patrick DesJarlait,
Red Lake Nation

contains the works of the great French Impressionists — Monet, Renoir, and Van Gogh. On my last visit to that city, however, I went in search of Ojibwe scrolls after hearing a rumor that some of them were housed in the Musée de l'Homme (Museum of Man). I did not find the scrolls; however, I did see one of the most extensive American Indian collections I had ever seen. It seemed so odd, almost bizarre, that I — an Ojibwe from northern Minnesota — would be in Paris viewing an American Indian exhibit. And as I stood before a glass-encased wampum belt of one of our Lenape relatives, I wondered aloud as to how and why the French came to possess such a sacred item. It did not belong there; it should have been among its own people.

The museums of Paris are filled with the stolen works resulting from colonialism — Greek, Roman, Italian, South American, Egyptian and North American art. And the art masters of Europe have captured their own cultures in sculpture, depicted their own wars in paintings, chronicled Christianity and cities and people. European art is a true reflection of European culture. The same could be said about indigenous art being a reflection of indigenous cultures. The aesthetic philosophy, medium, and music of the Ojibwe tell our story. Our art has been strongly influenced by the land upon which we live, by our encounters with animals, by the intense beauty of our natural surroundings, and by the water and sky and stars and all the wonders of the galaxy. Ojibwe art includes the beauty of our rock paintings, the floral designs of porcupine quill work, the more recent beadwork we adopted as a result of trading with Europeans, and the intricate design work on birch-bark containers (which was created by Ojibwe artisans using their teeth). Ojibwe art also includes the written language and petroglyphs (a form of compressed written language) our ancestors used to represent people, animals, and spirits. Our art is also in the colors that were symbolic of our Woodland homes and were expressive of the sacred directions — east (red), south (yellow), west (black), north (white), above (blue), below (green), here. Our ancestors used materials gathered from their surroundings — the hides and bone from deer, moose, rabbit, and other four-leggeds; feathers from eagles, partridge,

Churinga, bronze, sculpture by George Morrison, on the Fond du Lac Tribal and Community College Campus

Internationally recognized painter and sculptor George Morrison, Grand Portage band

turkey, and other winged creatures; birch bark, sweet grass, and black ash for baskets and other containers; clays from the earth for pottery; copper for jewelry; stone for pipes and effigies of various kinds. Moreover, our music and poetry were reflections of our natural surroundings, as represented in one of our spring songs (Vizenor, 1965, p. 41):

> *as my eyes*
> *look across the prairie*
> *i feel the summer*
> *in the spring*

There have been many influences on traditional Ojibwe art and music as a result of European colonization. Smaller birch-bark and sweet-grass containers became more popular because American tourists preferred them to larger containers. They are beautiful and do not take up an inordinate amount of space. Intricately beaded floral designs on deer-skin and moose-skin moccasins are sometimes sold as evening slippers in casino gift shops. Some people use beaded bingo daubers. *Dikinogan* (cradle boards) and lacrosse sticks have become works of art, adorning the walls of tribal centers and homes of Indian art collectors. Spirit paintings in woodland colors, done in acrylic and sometimes painted on birch bark or plain brown paper as well as on animal hides and canvas, adorn midwest art galleries. Age-old Ojibwe songs are rapidly being replaced with intertribal songs at our summer pow-wows. All of these changes are the result of our shifting and evolving culture.

The artwork of contemporary Ojibwe artists such as George Morrison is exhibited in galleries all over the world. One of Morrison's totem petroglyphs adorns Fond du Lac Tribal and Community College's forest campus. On the same campus, Truman Lowe's symbolic stream representation in stainless steel and river rocks serves as a sitting bench for students. Carl Gawboy's beautiful watercolors were recently on display in Sivertson's Art Gallery in Duluth, Minnesota. Patrick DesJarlait's paintings gained the artist a national reputation.

Art and music are a reflection of culture. As our culture has evolved with the influences of colonialism, our art and music have changed with the times. Where both will go in the future has yet to be determined, but it seems safe to say that Ojibwe art and music, however we define them, will continue so long as there are Ojibwe people on this earth.

Summary

I MENTIONED AT THE BEGINNING of the chapter my anger over the hypocrisy I felt at a showing of *Dear Finder*, a play about the perse-cution of the Jews by the Nazis during the Second World War. I was angry because we humans seem to revert to unfathomable cruelty over and over again, despite the lessons history provides; angry because those who attended the play put genocide in all its forms into the abstract, something that happened fifty years ago in Europe; angry because I know the history of the indigenous people of this country and know of our genocide; angry because we continue to live in a country that has not completely accepted its indigenous people as full and equal members of this society; angry because, as indigenous people, we have had to learn and be tested in schools and churches about the colonizer's creation stories, yet they do not know ours; angry because we have had to take years of Euro-American history and know of their migrations and they know little or nothing of ours; angry because we know the intricacies of the English language, in both its verbal and written forms, and they know little or nothing of ours; angry because we know of their great artists and art, and they know little or nothing about our artists or art.

But with all my anguish, I also have a great sense of hope. Because what is written here will be read by many non-Indians and because the photographs contained in this book will be viewed with great respect by the same people. And maybe as a result of this, they will begin to know our story — our creation story, our migrations, our language, our art. Perhaps, more importantly, Ojibwe young people who know little of their people's story will have access to this book, and they will begin to learn these things. That is the hope I have for the future.

Man in traditional dance outfit. Pow-wows remain an important part of Ojibwe life and a means of continuing the culture through music, dance, art, and language.

The Ojibwe burial grounds at Wisconsin Point, 1889

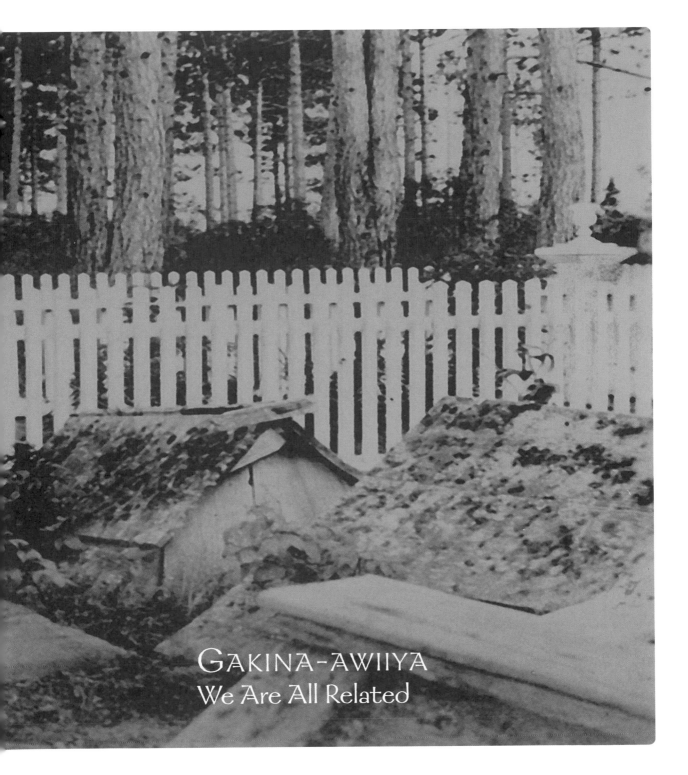

GAKINA-AWIIYA
We Are All Related

Our Elder Brothers: Relationship to the Land and Environment

A while back, I took my sons and granddaughter to Wisconsin Point, a spit of sand along Lake Superior's south shore just outside Superior, Wisconsin. Several generations of our ancestors had lived there. In 1914 an ownership dispute with the Interstate Railroad Company led to the removal of the Ojibwe, as well as the removal of many Ojibwe graves. Geologically, the land is new (three thousand years), created by wave action and sediment from the lake. In the span of human settlement of the area after the retreat of the last glacier, people from other tribal nations also called the area home. To this day, their spirits remind

Wisconsin Point on Lake Superior's south shore, where our Ojibwe ancestors lived until 1914, when the People and their burial grounds were removed.

Gravestone in St. Francis Cemetery, Superior, Wisconsin. The removed bodies of our Ojibwe ancestors lie buried in a mass grave along the bank of the Nemadji River. The stone reads: "Here lie the bodies removed from Indian cemetery on Wisconsin Point. Records of this cemetery association show the names of persons and locations of bodies."

us of their presence; pottery shards still wash out from the sand banks on the bay side of the point.

It was important that I take my sons and granddaughter to Wisconsin Point and tell them the story of that place, so they know it and pass it on to their children and their children's children. I was uncharacteristically direct in telling them why I took them to that sacred place, partially because they oftentimes do not understand the indirect and subtle way I dispense knowledge of these things. That is an old and traditional way of teaching things, and it is a way many of our young people do not understand. They needed to know their roles in protecting the area from any future development and of their responsibility to work to have the area forever set aside as a place to honor the Lake Superior Ojibwe.

Wisconsin Point is beautiful beyond description, with the sand and crashing surf of the lake on its north side and on the other, the bay, which was filled with loons, ducks, muskrat, and geese the evening we visited. To the west lay the hills of Duluth, Minnesota, where our ancestors once harvested animals and plants for sustenance and healing, and where long ago, boys who were coming of age sought visions that would give them life purpose. To the east the shores of the great lake stretched back beyond Madeline Island, the great ancestral homeland of the Ojibwe, and to the south were the forests of northern Wisconsin, all the way past the barrens of the St. Croix River valley, where our ancestors once hunted buffalo.

But there is more to that sacred land than its mere physical beauty, for hidden in and among a cleave of Norway pines, bowing and whispering to the winds of a strong nor'easter off the lake, lay the graves of our ancestors, the ones not removed. They are the ones who will remain there forever, the guardians of the story of that place. Our ancestors loved that place. They pleaded to remain, expressing it openly in a 1914 petition to President Woodrow Wilson (Peacock, 1998, p. 140):

We do grieve to contemplate the mere idea of this lovely nature nook, our beloved ancestral home, having warehouses and storehouses take the place of our homes, of cinders, covering our pure white sand, and our wild rose and harebell besprinkled grass, of groaning derricks and ore loaders, screeching souls, taking the place of our wonderful Norway pines, sighing out their organ music in the Wa-bun-e-no-din, the East wind, of fire-eyed engine monsters supplanting the mild eyed deer, of cats and rats taking the place of our noble game, in a word we remonstrate against the spoilation of this natural park, dignified by so many unusual charms.

The story of their eventual removal, as well the removal of the graves, is one of many in the tragedy that has marked Indian-white history, and it is something for which we still collectively grieve as a people.

When we left Wisconsin Point that evening, I drove us to St. Francis Cemetery in Old Town, Superior, Wisconsin, where the removed bodies of our ancestors lay buried in a mass grave along the banks of the Nemadji River. There, in an unkempt clay embankment that is sliding into the river, our ancestors wait to be taken home. And maybe because we, ourselves, have not made it our responsibility, their spirits have spoken to the spirits of the river, which is claiming them one by one and taking them back to the that sacred land, back to their homes.

The wild white rose,
Wisconsin Point

A Chapter Road Map

JUST AS OUR ANCESTORS KNEW the interrelationships of things and lived their lives as brothers and sisters with all the animates and inanimates of the earth, the Ojibwe of today are slowly returning to these traditional values. These ways are ingrained in our ancestral memory. This chapter is about the relationship of the Ojibwe to everything animate and inanimate. We begin with a description of the Ojibwe perspective on the natural world, as keepers of harmony and balance, the collective spirit of places, and of ancestors. We describe the original lands of the Anishinabe nation. We then move on to the impact of European contact on the land and environment, paying specific attention to the fur trade. We counter the Ojibwe belief in elder brothers (plants and animals) with the European philosophy of control over the natural environment and of resource management. A section is devoted to the period of American expansionism, of the treaty period, and of the losing of our traditional homelands because of the encroachment of white settlement. Contemporary issues of land and environment are discussed, including the influences of self-determination on traditional gathering (hunting and fishing rights), the Voight court decision of 1985, the U.S. Supreme Court decision of 1999, and the land and environmental issues of the day. Ojibwe leaders' perspectives on these issues are offered. Finally, we take a hopeful look into the future, at a rekindling of the Ojibwe world view of this great Mother earth, of plans, and of visions and visionaries.

The Ojibwe Perspective of the Natural World

There is nothing romantic about the notion that humans are keepers of the natural world. We are the keepers, as were our ancestors before us. It is as simple as that. Simon Ortiz (Acoma Pueblo) reminded us of the responsibility adults have to model this behavior to young people, thereby passing down this tradition through the generations (Bruchac, 1983, p. 187):

WAAWAASHKESHI (deer)

My Father's Song

Wanting to say things,
I miss my father tonight,
His voice, the slight catch,
the depth from his thin chest,
the tremble of emotion
in something he has just said
to his son, his song:

> *We planted corn one Spring at Acu-*
> *we planted several times*
> *but this particular time*
> *I remember the soft damp sand*
> *in my hand.*

> *My father had stopped at one point*
> *to show me an overturned furrow;*
> *the plowshare had unearthed*
> *the burrow nest of a mouse*
> *in the soft moist sand.*

> *Very gently, he scooped up tiny pink animals*
> *into the palm of his hand*
> *and told me to touch them.*
> *We took them to the edge*
> *of the field and put them in the shade*
> *of a sand moist clod.*

> *I remember the very softness*
> *of cool and warm sand and tiny alive mice*
> *and my father saying things.*

There are many Ojibwe stories that relate our responsibility as keepers of the natural world. One such story tells of when the hoofed animals (moose, caribou, and deer) disappeared. Without these creatures offering themselves as sustenance, our ancestors' food supply was quickly diminished. It happened that an owl found the hoofed animals living in the north, content and happy and protected by the crows. Reporting to the Ojibwe, the owl showed them the animals' whereabouts. When the Ojibwe tried to retrieve the animals, they were attacked by the crows. A battle was waged. It lasted for days and was without a victor. Soon the Ojibwe asked for an end to the battle. All the while, the animals made no attempt to escape from the crows and seemed content and indifferent to their rescue. When asked why they did not wish to escape, the animals replied that the

ASIGAAWANIDIWAAD
GAAGAAGIWAG
(they flock together ravens)

There is nothing romantic about the notion of humans being keepers of the natural world. We are the keepers, as were our ancestors before us.

crows treated them better than the humans did. Humans had wasted their remains, they said, and had let their bones lie scattered about in a careless way and had thus dishonored them. Only after the Ojibwe promised to honor the animals in life and death did the hoofed animals return to the land of the Ojibwe.

Harmony and balance with the natural world are an integral part of the Ojibwe way of being. If we harvest too many fish in one season, there will be fewer fish to eat in the future. If we cut down too many trees, the land will become barren, and regrowth will occur with brush and trees of less usefulness. If we scatter the earth with our refuse, junked cars, and abandoned appliances, the collective beauty of a place will suffer. That is the essential wisdom of the traditional way of viewing the natural world. This wisdom is really quite simple and direct: respect the plants and all the inanimates, which were the first in the creation of this earth. We need them for food and medicine and for their natural beauty. Respect our elder brothers the animals. We need them for the examples they offer on how to live, for food, and for spiritual matters. Our survival is dependent on their survival. Have respect for all things (Axtell and Aragon, 1997, p. 208-209):

Have respect for rain, the snow — the weather. The weather is something the Creator gave us. It's a gift. He gives us water to revitalize us. It gives us a refreshing feeling.

Have kindness for all living things. Not just the animals. I mean the plants and trees, and the grass — all have life. When I was young I used to like to shoot things. Especially when I got my first gun. My grandaunt, who was a medicine woman, gave me this teaching. We were walking one time and we came upon a rattlesnake. I got scared. I started to pick up a rock and she stopped my hand. She went over and broke off a willow switch about three feet long and left some leaves on the end of it. She took that switch and chased the snake away.

"Let him live. He belongs on this land like we do. He was made by the Creator just like we were."

Just as Horace Axtell, a Nez Perce elder, reminded us of the necessity of respecting the natural things of this earth, so we must be reminded that all the things around us have a collective spirit. Acknowledging the collective nature of things is another essential part of our way of being. Some time ago I traveled to Red Cliff, Wisconsin, the home of my father and grandparents and of their parents. I am often called to that place of our great Ojibwe homeland when I am in need of solace and reflection. This particular time I stopped at Bear Landing, just off the highway in Red Cliff, and walked a pathway to a bench my great-grandfather had built overlooking the blue of Lake Superior. There, off in the distance, lay the Apostle Islands — Hermit, Oak, Basswood, and Madeline Islands. I sat on the bench my ancestor had built many, many years ago, and I was overcome with a sense of awe and wonderment at the collective spirit of that place. It was all around me — in the buzzing of insects and the chattering of birds, in the hush of grasses as they bowed to the wind, in the lapping sounds of the water on the rocks, in the blue of sky and the sparkle of sun off the waves, and in my own muffled voice. I could feel the spirits of my father and great-grandparents sitting on the bench with me that day, and it was as though I saw the world with the same sense of wonder that children, like my granddaughters, see the world with. The past, present, and future, all were a part of the collective spirit of that place.

Traditional Nationhood

The traditional homelands of the Ojibwe were not populated solely by one nation. Both the eastward (as attested in the Wallum Olum of our Lenape ancestors) and westward migrations of the Ojibwe show fluid rather than permanent nation boundaries. What we know as Ojibwe country today resulted from the recent westward expansion. This expansion was both voluntary (see Warren's description of the westward migration) and a result of warfare, in which the Ojibwe and their Lenape relatives were pushed west by the Iroquois Federation. This most recent migration continued well into the eighteenth century. Other people — the Dakota, Sauk, Fox, Huron, Menominee, Ottawa, and Potawatomi — also included this land as part of their nations. To be sure, our ancestors engaged in armed struggles with other tribal nations for the use of the land; however, international boundaries as we know them today did not exist in those times. In a sense, land was not something to possess and govern. Land was a place to live and to be a part of. And it was a great stretch of land, covering portions of Canada and the United States (Ojibwe Curriculum Committee, 1973, p. 4):

The homeland was immense, stretching in a great curve from the northern reaches of the plains to the southeastern shores of the Great Lakes. In Canada it extended from central Saskatchewan to southern Ontario, and in the United States it included the northeastern corner of North Dakota, northern Minnesota and Wisconsin, most of Michigan, and part of northern Ohio. The Ojibwe regarded their land as a gift from the Great Spirit to their people, and it belonged to everyone in the tribe. They lived on it and loved it and resisted any who tried to drive them from it.

Although our ancestors identified who they were primarily by dodaim (clan membership) and then by community, there was a sense of tribal unity, as one people, in those traditional times. This sense was

Bear image, representing the bear *dodaim* (clan), painted on a rock in Little Sand Bay, just east of the Red Cliff Reservation, Wisconsin

Beaver hooked rug, Grand Portage Monument, 1920

strong, especially in times of war, when runners would be sent to far-flung Ojibwe villages to call for warriors to join in struggles against our traditional enemies. Moreover, a larger sense of identity with other Lenape people was shown in the early 1800s when Tecumseh, a Shawnee, and his brother, Tentswatawa (the Prophet), tried to unite with the Ojibwe, Ottawa, and others against the invasion of their homelands by white settlers.

This larger sense of tribal nationhood stands in stark contrast to the autonomous reservations that are the remaining pieces of our former homelands. Today, many Ojibwe people tend to identify with and have allegiance to a community or a reservation rather than their clan. We are from L'anse, Bad River, Red Lake, or Turtle Mountain. Today we identify who we are by saying we are Leech Lakers, or Red Lakers, or Bad Riverites, or from LCO. Others identify with specific communities on reservations — Naytahwaush, White Earth village, Waubun, Roy Lake, Redby, Ponemah, or Sawyer. Some of us carefully guard who can and who cannot be members of our communities through new customs and new rules — blood quantum, residency requirements, enrollment documents, and the like. JOM Indians (those enrolled and who have one-fourth or more Indian blood) and Title IX (those who can claim Indian heritage through grandparents) count who is Indian by federally determined criteria. Moreover, we have drawn distinctions based on state boundaries. Some Wisconsin Ojibwe reservations do not accept Minnesota Ojibwe heritage in considering tribal enrollment, and vice versa. Ojibwe who are enrolled on one reservation and live on another reservation are sometimes referred to as "outsiders." This fractured sense of who we are as a people seems to be a direct result of colonization, of the acceptance of the new labels (enrolled, nonenrolled, urban, reservation, etc.) adopted by the federal government and by ourselves, of the reservation system, and of our own sense of displacement and alienation in this country. This sense was tragically expressed by Black Elk, who saw his own people, the Oglala, falter (Neihardt, 1932, p. 270):

And I, to whom so great a vision was given in my youth, — you see me now a pitiful old man who has done nothing, for the nation's hoop is broken and scattered. There is no center any longer, and the sacred tree is dead.

This limited perception of who we are, however, is slowly changing. Throughout Ojibwe country there is a growing awareness of tribal identity based on being *Anishinabe* and a decreasing identification with individual reservations or tribal communities.

Contact with Europeans

Early contact with the French, and later with the English and the Americans, led to profound changes in Ojibwe country, which affected nearly all aspects of traditional life, including tribal boundaries, cultures, perspectives toward the natural environment, political systems, and economies. With the advent of trade goods resulting from the exchange of furs, age-old Ojibwe ways were forever changed. The iron kettle soon replaced the bark container, and the knowledge of the old skills used to make the containers became but a foggy memory in some communities. Woolen blankets and clothing supplanted furs, which had once been used for clothing. Beads replaced much of the porcupine quill work in crafts. The steel ax took the place of the stone ax. Warren (1974) noted, "Their clay kettles, pots, and dishes were exchanged for copper and brass utensils." The wholesale slaughter of the animals, our elder brothers, began. Their hides were exchanged for trade goods.

The Effects of the Fur Trade on Land and Environment

Perhaps no single item affected tribal boundaries more than the introduction of the firearm, which was among the first of the trade goods. Tribes who were introduced to firearms soon had an upper hand with their indigenous neighbors. The Iroquois traded with the Dutch for guns and then used their superior numbers and weaponry

American Fur Trading Post at Fond du Lac

to drive out the Huron from the region of uppermost New York and the St. Lawrence River Valley in the early 1600s (Ojibwe Curriculum Committee, 1973). The Huron fled as far west as eastern Minnesota. The Ottawa were then pushed west, where they came upon other similarly displaced Potawatomi, Sauk, and Menominee. Soon the easternmost Ojibwe fell prey to the Naudoway, the Iroquois, and were pushed west to Sault Ste. Marie and the Lake Nipigon area.

Within a brief time, however, the Ojibwe also came to trade with the French and acquired the gun, which they used as they continued the movement west, where they soon displaced the Dakota. For a period of time, the Ojibwe also served as intermediaries with other tribes (Ojibwe Curriculum Committee, 1973, p. 11):

Here, also, the Ojibwe prospered as go-betweens in the trade between the French and the tribes farther to the west. These were mainly Cree and Assiniboin, both of whom were at war with the Dakota. The northern Ojibwe, especially the Monsoni, had strong ties with the Cree and took their side in the continuing war with the Dakota. Meanwhile, the Ojibwe of Chequamegon, who were still allies of the Dakota, sometimes joined in expeditions against these northern enemies. But for the most part the Ojibwe were neutral and could travel safely in the country between the warring tribes. This included the chain of lakes and streams that leads west from Lake Superior along what is now the international border.

The gun replaced the bow and arrow, resulting in the Ojibwe having superior fire power over the Dakota, their traditional enemies. The use of this weaponry contributed heavily to the Dakota removal from Michigan, Wisconsin, and much of Minnesota. Moreover, with a gun, the Ojibwe spent less time hunting and more time devoted to gathering furs to trade for more goods.

Perhaps more tragically, one of the first trade goods introduced into Ojibwe country was alcohol, which is still devastating in many communities. An early Ojibwe woman's account of the first interactions between Indians and non-Indians includes trade for alcohol, first with the French and British and later with the *Chemokoman* (long knives, or Americans) (Kohl, 1985, p. 371):

At first the Indians did not love the Yaganash [English]. He brought with him much iskotewabo (fire-water) with him. The Frenchman had also fire-water but not so much as the Englishman. Hence things have now grown much worse in the country. When the Indian had many furs, he drank much fire-water. And my grandfather, who was old, very old, old, often told me this sorrowful story. He often told me that more than one-half of the Indians died of this "whiskey water."

The fur trade also influenced the political make-up of communities. For the most part, the French respected the *dodaim* system of community leadership and organization. This was not true, however, for the British and later the Americans. Both the British and American traders were soon heavily involved in community governance, sometimes appointing chiefs and other leaders. People who became leaders were the ones who could speak English and who could better interact with and cooperate with the colonizers. Age-old ways of selecting leaders were forever changed. Christian missionaries became dominant forces in

Firearms and alcohol, acquired as a result of the fur trade, heavily influenced the Ojibwe way of life.

Ojibwe communities and were closely followed by Indian agents, who often ruled over communities with an iron hand.

During the 1840s, the federal government tried to remove Ojibwe people from their homelands around Lake Superior and force them west to Minnesota Territory. To counter this, Ojibwe delegates to Washington in 1849 brought with them this symbolic petition.
The animals represent the Ojibwe dodaim (clans). Other images are of the People's beloved homelands, with the lines connecting the hearts and eyes to the wild rice lakes, symbolic of the group's unity of purpose.

Treaty Diagram, from a drawing by Seth Eastman of a birch bark pictograph

The fur trade resulted in exploitation of the fur-bearing animals of the region, especially the beaver, whose fur was prized among the upper classes of Europe. A gauge of the growth of the fur industry was the continuing westward push of our ancestors toward more and better fur-bearing country and the building of fur posts. Ojibwe journeys to Montreal to trade with the French were soon shortened when the fur companies built posts at Detroit, Mackinaw, Sault Ste. Marie, LaPointe, Grand Portage, and Fond du Lac. Animals paid the price for the fur trade, and when they were depleted in the northern and westernmost areas of Ojibwe country and styles in Europe changed by the 1870s, the fur trade came to a halt, after more than two hundred years. The Ojibwe were left destitute, without a means of survival, and many became dependent upon the federal government for their basic needs.

Trade was the factor that contributed to peace between non-Indians and the Ojibwe and explains why the Ojibwe did not offer much armed resistance to the taking of their lands by non-Indians. This was described by Ray (1974) in *Indians in the Fur Trade*:

In the broadest sense, it was a partnership for the exploitation of resources. Although it was not an equal partnership, nor one in which the other group always held the upper hand, at no time before 1870 would it have served the interests of one party to destroy the other since by doing so the aggressors would have been deprived of the supplies of goods or furs or provisions.

Beaver, Noel DuCharme, painting, 1981

Ojibwe women and children guarding corn from blackbirds, 1862. Ojibwe people were encouraged to become farmers.

Differing Philosophies of the Ojibwe and Non-Indians

The belief in harmony and balance with nature was fundamental to traditional Ojibwe culture. Animals were regarded as elder brothers and put before man in the order of things. This was true with many indigenous people (Cuduto and Bruchac, 1991, p. xviii):

Native North Americans see themselves as part of nature, not apart from it. Their stories use natural images to teach about relationships between people, and between people, animals and the rest of the Earth. To the native peoples of North America, what was done to a frog or a deer, to a tree, a rock or a river, was done to a brother or a sister.

Plants, and other animates and inanimates, were regarded as possessing spirit. How is it these fundamental values were compromised during the period of the fur trade? What caused the exploitation of the animals for economic gain? Was the urge to have superior goods and firearms, and in some instances alcohol, too great? To be sure, traditional Ojibwe values were severely tested, and there was a period of time when we were partners in animal exploitation as much as the colonizers. Yet our values survived the fur trade. Perhaps it took the near extermination of our animal brothers, and the resulting impoverishment as a result of the decline in the fur trade, for us to be reminded of our interrelationships with all the things of this earth and of the need for harmony and balance. The fact that these values remain viable today is a testament to their strength.

The Effects of American Expansionism

While the fur trade became the conduit for intercourse between the colonizers and the indigenous people of this part of the country, the need for land for the waves of European settlers led to a different relationship. Part of the resulting conflict between Indian people and the colonizers was a result of their differing philosophies of property ownership. Euro-Americans believe in individual ownership of property. This philosophy runs counter to that of many indigenous cultures, where people believe that land is something that cannot be owned, bought, or sold. Land was something to use, to live on, and to be a part of. The indigenous people became unequal participants in the taking of their traditional homelands by the colonizers as a result of a multiplicity of factors, including their lesser numbers, inferior weaponry, misplaced trust in the colonizers' good intentions, and the devastation of their numbers by the diseases introduced from Europe (Zinn, 1980, p. 16):

The Indian population of 10 million that was in North America when Columbus came would ultimately be reduced to less than a million. Huge numbers of Indians would die from diseases introduced by the whites. A Dutch traveler in New Netherlands wrote in 1656 that "the Indians . . . affirm, that before the arrival of Christians, and before the smallpox broke out amongst them, they were ten times as numerous as they now are."

The Treaty Period (1781-1927)

With a few notable exceptions, our Ojibwe ancestors offered little armed resistance to those who took their lands, and they were unwilling partners in a series of treaties, purchases, and agreements from 1781 to 1927, which resulted in the establishment of reserves in both Canada and the United States and the ceding of most of the traditional homelands. A crucial element of the treaties was that they affirmed the government-to-government relationship between tribes and the American government. This notion of tribal sovereignty recognized Indian nations as sovereign, dependent nations within the United States. This concept is critical to understanding tribal-federal relations and is what separates Indian people from other citizens of this country. Some of the early treaties and agreements include (Ojibwe Curriculum Committee, 1973):

— **1781** Treaty between the British and various bands of the Ojibwe for land along the Niagara River between Lake Erie and Lake Ontario, including the Canadian side of Niagara Falls
  — **1781** British purchase of Mackinaw Island
  — **1783** Missisauga band cedes territory along the northern shore of Lake Ontario to the British

Ojibwe lands ceded by the various treaties with the federal government.

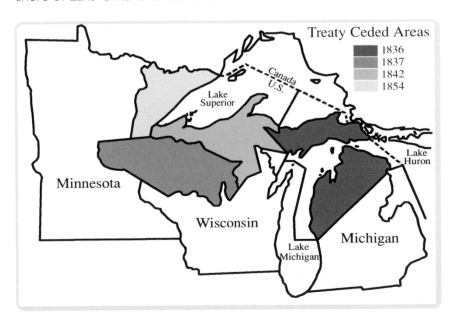

Some Ojibwe settled in the prairie regions of North Dakota and Montana, living on the Turtle Mountain and Rocky Boy Reservations.

— **1795** Treaty of Greenville cedes all of southern and eastern Ohio to the United States as a result of the Indian defeat (including some bands of Ojibwe) at the Battle of Fallen Timbers

— **1805, 1807,** and **1817** Treaties cede land in northern Ohio and southern Michigan

— **1819** Treaty in which the Ojibwe cede the area around the valley of the Saginaw River and shores of Saginaw Bay in Lower Michigan

— **1821** Remaining Ottawa and Ojibwe sell the rest of their land in southwestern Michigan and move northward

— **1816–33** A group of tribes, calling themselves the United Nation of Chippewa, Ottawa, and Potawatomi, living in southern Ohio, give up claims east of the Mississippi River and sign an **1833** treaty promising them land on the western plains.

The Ojibwe heartland was taken in a series of treaties and agreements between 1836 and 1867 (Ojibwe Curriculum Committee, 1973, p. 28):

The years between 1836 and 1867 were a time of great change and sorrow for most of the Ojibwe people. Pressure upon them increased from all sides, and within this third of a century the white man took possession of the core of the Anishinabe land. . . . This included all of the area bordering Lake Superior, most of what remained bordering Lake Huron, northern Wisconsin, Michigan, and Minnesota, and the plains of the Red River Valley, reaching into the northeastern corner of what is now North Dakota.

A list of these treaties and agreements follows (Ojibwe Curriculum Committee, 1973):

— **1836** Ottawa and Ojibwe sell the northwestern part of Lower Michigan and eastern half of Upper Michigan

— **1836** British make an agreement with the Ottawa and Ojibwe living on Manitoulin Island and other islands in Lake Huron to allow other Indians to settle there as part of an unsuccessful effort to create an exclusive Indian territory

— **1837** Treaty with the Pillager, Red Lake, Mississippi, Fond du Lac, and Chequamegon bands cedes lands in Wisconsin and central Minnesota (the 1999 United States Supreme Court decision that upheld the Ojibwe right to hunt, fish, and gather in these areas was based on this treaty)

— **1842** Treaty cedes the rich copper and iron areas in northern Michigan

— **1847** Treaty with the Pillager and Mississippi bands for tracts of land in central Minnesota to be used as reserves for removed Winnebago and Menominee tribes (the Menominee refuse to move, preferring to stay near Green Bay; the Winnebago slowly move back to Wisconsin)

— **1850** British acquire all of the land north of Lake Huron from the Ottawa River on the east to Lake Superior on the west, which includes most of the land north of Lake Superior

— **1854** Treaty with the Mississippi, Lake Superior, and Bois Forte bands at LaPointe, Wisconsin, cedes the land along the western side of Lake Superior between Fond du Lac in Minnesota to the border with Canada

— **1855** Treaty with the Mississippi, Pillager, and Lake Winnebigoshish bands cedes lands around the Mississippi headwaters

— **1864** Treaty with Pembina and Red Lake bands cedes the Red River Valley, an area considered one of the richest agricultural areas in the United States

— **1866** The last major treaty between the Ojibwe and the United States government in which the Bois Forte band cedes a small piece of land in northern Minnesota just south of the Rainy River

— **1869** United States purchases a large tract of land in northern Minnesota from the Red Lake band

— **1871** Ojibwe and Cree cede much of southern Manitoba

— **1871** Ojibwe around Lake Manitoba cede another large tract of land in southern Manitoba

— **1873** Ojibwe lose southern Ontario north of the border with Minnesota through a land cession

— **1874–75** Ojibwe and Cree lose all of southeastern Saskatchewan and the land surrounding Lake Winnipeg by treaty cession

— **1905, 1910,** and **1929** Canada acquires through treaty huge tracts of Ojibwe land bordering Hudson Bay.

Ojibwe Resistance to the Loss of Their Homelands

Only in a few instances did the Ojibwe take up arms to preserve their homelands. Some joined the coalition led by Tecumseh, a Shawnee (one of our Lenape relatives), who tried to forge an alliance of tribes to oppose the taking of Indian lands. Tecumseh had urged Indians to cast off the ways of the white man and return to their old ways. An expedition of Chequamegon warriors (Ojibwe Curriculum Committee, 1973) left for Detroit to join in the struggle only to find that Tecumseh had already been defeated at the Wabash River in Indiana. Many other Ojibwe, however, fought in that losing struggle.

In 1885, a small band of Ojibwe, led by Stone Child or Little Stone Man (erroneously referred to as "Rocky Boy"), aligned themselves with the Métis and Cree, in what became known as the Riel Rebellion (so called because it was led by a mixed-blood named

Louis Riel burial site, St. Boniface, Manitoba.

Chief Bugonaygeshig led the last armed struggle of American Indians against U.S. armed forces at Sugar Point, Leech Lake, in 1898.

Louis Riel), against Canadian expansionism into Saskatchewan and the land around Lake Winnipeg. After they were defeated by Canadian forces, they were forced into years of a wandering existence, with some of our Cree relatives finally being granted a small reserve at Rocky Boy, Montana.

The last armed conflict between Ojibwe warriors and troops of the United States government, a struggle led by Bugonaygeshig (Hole in the Day), took place in 1898 at Sugar Point, on the south shore of Leech Lake, Minnesota.

A Conspiracy that Led to the Death of Four Hundred Ojibwe Men, Women, and Children

Many of us would like to think that our Ojibwe ancestors were never the victims of overt genocide to the extent of what happened to other indigenous nations of this continent (the forced march of the Cherokee, the death marches of the Northern Cheyenne, the massacres of Indian people at Sand Creek and Wounded Knee), but history tells another story. A plot hatched by government officials was directly responsible for the deaths of four hundred Ojibwe men, women, and children, according to figures recorded by Buffalo, a leader from LaPointe. Because earlier efforts by the government to get Wisconsin and Michigan Ojibwe to move to northwestern Minnesota Territory had failed, the idea was to induce the Ojibwe of Lake Superior to come to Sandy Lake (in central Minnesota) late in fall under a guise of issuing annuity payments and rations, thereby trapping them during the winter. More than three thousand Ojibwe gathered at Sandy Lake in early October 1850. Exposure, starvation, and disease led to the deaths of 170, and another 270 died on their way home (Clifton, 1987, p. 1):

Throughout the fall of 1850, four officials of Zachery Taylor's administration conspired to lure the Lake Superior Chippewa Indians away from their lands in Northern Wisconsin and Michigan's Upper Peninsula. Two of these officials, Secretary of the Interior Thomas Ewing and Commissioner of Indian Affairs Orlando Brown, provided the initial approval for the plan, but they did not remain in office long enough to witness its disastrous results. The others, Minnesota Territory's governor, Alexander Ramsey, and Sub-Agent John Watrous, were directly involved as prime movers from start to end. By moving the place of the annual annuity payments to a new temporary sub-agency at Sandy Lake on the east bank of the Mississippi [LaPointe, Wisconsin, was the usual annuity site] and by stalling the delivery of annuity goods and money, they planned to trap the Chippewa by winter weather, thus forcing them to remain at this remote, isolated location.

The Ojibwe who gathered at Sandy Lake soon found out there was no annuity awaiting them. Illness (dysentery, possibly cholera, and measles), hunger (the scant rations soon ran out), and exposure took their toll. The encampment finally broke up on December 3, 1850, and the survivors headed home.

Annuity payment in 1871 in Wisconsin. Payments were usually made at LaPointe.

Leech Lake delegation in Washington D.C., 1899, (l–r) Be-miss, Paul Bonga, William Bonga, Jim Fisher, Gay-she-gwanay-aush, Gegwejiwebinung, Gimewuanc, Ne-gon-e-bin-ais, Ta-da-gah-mah-shi, Wabununi

The Allotment Act and Other Ways Ojibwe Land Was Taken

My father told me of a time when he went to check his fish nets and happened to stop on Raspberry Island, which lies several miles offshore in Lake Superior. Raspberry Island is a hauntingly beautiful place, with old stands of Norway and white pine, an abandoned sandstone quarry, and a shoreline covered with rocks and driftwood. At its southern tip lives a family of eagles, who roost majestically and remind us of our place in the order of things. This island is part of the Apostle Islands, once our traditional homeland, and it is a sacred place.

My father stopped to walk along the shoreline and wonder about the beauty of that place. A short time later a National Park Service boat pulled alongside, and the driver asked him why he was there. And my father told me of the deep, historical anger he felt at being asked that question because he knew that this was once part of his grandmother's allotment land. He told me of how the land had been lost years ago. Back then, he said, the Indian Service would send letters to allottees (those who held land in trust from the federal government either as individuals or as a group of family members), telling them there was a buyer for the land or, in this particular case, that the land was being taken back by the federal government as part of the establishment of the Apostle Islands National Seashore. In those days, if Indian people did not respond, the federal government took their lack of response as a "yes" to sell the land. This was at a time when Indian people were powerless to fight for their rights. They had no money for attorneys to push their cause, and tribal governments operated at the whim of Indian agents. Moreover,

it was customary for Ojibwe people not to respond to matters in which they disagreed. Silence was not a "yes," but a form of disapproval.

My father responded in the old way learned from his father. He shook his head in disgust and walked away: *Mind-a-way* (the Ojibwe way of showing anger and disgust, like being too angry to respond). That is how we Ojibwe feel when we are asked what we are doing in places that were once ours.

My father was an unwilling participant. The taking of his grandmother's land was a result of the Dawes Allotment Act of 1887, which allotted parcels of reservation lands for agricultural purposes. The remainder of the reservation lands were sold to white settlers as a way of opening up more land for settlement and as a way to get at the rich timber reserves or minerals on reservations. Indians who were declared "competent" by the federal government were allowed to sell their allotments. That is how many of our reservations ended up looking like patchwork quilts, with small parcels of Indian land surrounded by individually owned non-Indian land. Today, many of these remaining Indian parcels have many individual Indian heirs (as an example, I am an heir to allotment land for which there are more than three hundred other heirs). It is impossible to use such land for anything, since agreement is needed from each heir in order to use it.

There were other ways, too, in which the land was lost. Railroads laid tracks across reservations and acquired large sections of land as a result of condemnation. Timber barons used the allotment act to open up large sections of reservation land for clear cutting. Mineral seekers convinced the federal government to acquire, through treaty, large sections of Indian land to develop copper and iron mines in Upper Michigan and northern Minnesota. Throughout most of this period, our ancestors were powerless to stop the disintegration of their land base and, subsequently, their ways of being.

Swan River Logging camp, Chippewa National Forest, 1900–1902

A graphic representation of the policy of assimilation by the federal government, churches and business interests

Assimilation Dress, Laura Heit

Denial of Traditional Gathering Practices

Although our ancestors were unequal participants in the treaties in which we lost our land, one thing they did insist on in nearly every treaty was that they retain their right to hunt, fish, and gather in the territories ceded (land sold to or taken by) to the federal government. This practice is similar to the specific language put in contemporary land transactions when a seller puts an easement into the purchase agreement. It is a property right, and therein lies the fundamental disagreement in many treaty rights cases. Indians see hunting, fishing, and gathering in territory ceded to the federal government as a property right, or rights retained by treaty. States who have fought against Indian treaty rights see it as unfair "special" rights of Indians. But treaty rights are something we retained; they were not special rights given to Indians.

Furthermore, all the factors resulting in loss of power by our ancestors — the impoverishment resulting from the collapse of the fur trade economy, the loss of traditional homelands, the prohibition of traditional Ojibwe spiritual practices, the forced removal of children to boarding and mission schools, and the dependence on the federal government for day-to-day survival — meant most of the decisions on reservations were made by non-Indian government agents. Moreover, states soon began to assert their jurisdiction over reservation lands, prosecuting crimes and enforcing their game and fish laws. Ojibwe people were powerless to fight this encroachment on their sovereignty. States eventually denied the Ojibwe access to hunt, fish, and gather in the territories ceded as a result of treaties. In addition, on many reservations, state game wardens arrested and prosecuted Indians for hunting and fishing on their own small parcels of remaining Indian land. This practice continued well into the 1980s.

With the encroachment of mining and other industry, Ojibwe land became a dumping ground for toxic wastes. Copper and iron mining devastated the earth, leaving gaping holes. The toxic chemicals required to process these minerals traveled freely and dangerously across reservation land. Paper mills dumped millions of tons of mercury and dioxin into rivers and streams. The water from rivers was diverted for power plants, and traditional ricing areas were forever ruined. The fish from the lakes became toxic, and tribal people became the subjects of toxic studies. Even today, acid rain continues to have an adverse effect on the wild rice crop.

And all through this painful period of history our Ojibwe grandparents and parents waited for better times. We are a patient people. We knew that times would get better.

The Indian Reorganization Act

The deep despair on reservations did not go unnoticed in eastern social and political circles, and sympathy for the indigenous people grew rapidly, eventually leading to congressional action (Ojibwe Curriculum Committee, 1973, p. 43):

In 1928 Congress directed an independent commission to make a full-scale study of Indian policy. The findings of this commission, known as the Merriam Report, suggested a whole new direction in government dealings with Indian people. This change was carried out through the Indian Reorganization Act of 1934. The act ended allotment and further sales of Indian land and provided for the buying back of some tribal lands. It also set up machinery for organizing tribal governments on the model of white democratic institutions.

The Indian Reorganization Act (IRA) led to the formation of modern tribal governments, as we know them today, with a limited form of self-governance and self-determination. Some bands organized into confederated organizations, such as Leech Lake, White Earth, Mille Lacs Lake, Boise Forte, Grand Portage, and Fond du Lac Reservations, under the Minnesota Chippewa Tribe. Other Ojibwe didn't, including St. Croix, Mole Lake, Lac View Desert, Sault Ste. Marie, and Grand Traverse. The IRA eventually led to the most sweeping changes in Ojibwe country since the colonization of our homelands by Europeans and paved the way for the modern tribal communities we know today.

Contemporary Ojibwe Society

The reform brought on by the Indian Reorganization Act was short-lived and was followed by a brief Termination Period, whereby Congressional sentiment swung toward the termination of the federal status of some tribes, including the Menominee of Wisconsin. During this period, it was felt that the only way to ensure the full inclusion of American Indians in American society was to end federal oversight and federal status, and to allow tribal people to fully assimilate into mainstream society. Education reform ended, with tribal language and culture programs discontinued. The Bureau of Indian Affairs, however, maintained its strong influence over Indian affairs, and attempted to control the actions of tribal governments through policy declarations, decrees, rules, regulations, and its limited monetary resources. For the most part, tribes were powerless against both federal and state actions, and the notion of tribal self-determination fell by the wayside.

Protests such as the Winter Dam occupation of August 1–3, 1971, by the American Indian Movement (AIM) served to awaken public awareness to the need for changes in the way the country was dealing with Indian issues.

Anti-mining demonstrators on the Bad River Reservation, Wisconsin. Mining interests attempted to transport chemicals across the reservation to be used in copper mining.

Self-Determination

But soon the winds of change began to blow again throughout Indian country. In 1961, Indian leaders met in Chicago and issued a "Declaration of Indian Purpose," which set the groundwork for what would soon become the Indian self-determination movement. The civil rights and social reform movement of the 1960s began to affect the lives of tribal people. The War on Poverty, and its subsequent federal programs, particularly the Community Action Programs, led to the development of tribal infrastructures and the delivery of services in Ojibwe communities through tribal governments. The American Indian Movement, which began as a foot patrol to monitor police brutality against Indians in Minneapolis's Indian neighborhoods, was a leader in awakening the public consciousness to the need for changes in the way the country was dealing with Indian matters. Although their militant tactics were sometimes seen as too harsh for some reservation Indians, AIM received media coverage (through takeovers of area Bureau of Indian Affairs offices, the Department of Interior in Washington D.C., and the hamlet at Wounded Knee, South Dakota), and this publicity served to put the plight of Indian people on the public policy agenda. The Kennedy Report of 1968 led to sweeping changes in Indian education and Indian health, and issued a cry for tribal self-determination. A host of Congressional actions ensued, including the Indian Civil Rights Act of 1968, Indian Education Act of 1972, and Indian Self-Determination and Education Assistance Act of 1975. The latter act was perhaps the most sweeping of all Congressional actions, because for the first time the federal government formally acknowledged the need for self-determination throughout Indian country, and gave tribes limited self-determination by allowing them to contract for services formerly provided by federal agencies, including the Bureau of Indian Affairs and Indian Public Health Service. The growth in tribal governments, and the infrastructures to support the delivery of services, were a direct result of the self-determination policy.

Indian protesters in
Washington D.C., 1998

The Treaty Rights Movement

With the growing economic and political influence of tribal governments,
tribes began to assert their influence in courts, seeking to reclaim the
hunting, fishing and gathering rights guaranteed them in treaties. These
actions were met with stiff opposition by local units of government, and
states, which often enjoined against tribes in lengthy and expensive
lawsuits in attempts to stop tribes from exercising their treaty rights.
Federal court decisions, however, have favored tribes. Perhaps the most
important decision affecting Ojibwe country was what today has
become known as the Voight decision of 1985, which upheld the rights
of Ojibwe tribes in Wisconsin to hunting, fishing and gathering rights.
Individual tribal members, exercising treaty rights under tribal natural
resources regulations, began to again engage in the traditional spring
spear fishing harvest. These harvests were met with strong and
vehement protests by so-called sportsmen's groups, resort owners,
anti-treaty rights supporters, and racists. Tribal spear fishermen were
protected by both state and tribal wardens in the exercise of their
treaty rights, all the while being subject to blatant racist attacks, including
cries to "Save the fish, kill the Indian," and "timber niggers." In the end,

March 24, 1999—A good day in Indian country
Supreme Court issues favorable treaty ruling

Headline from *Masinaigan* announcing the 1999 treaty decision of the U.S. Supreme Court regarding treaty rights

however, the protest only served to strengthen public support for Indian treaty rights, as anti-treaty rights supporters were often branded as reactionaries and racists.

States continue to fight tribal treaty rights, and in one instance did so all the way to the federal Supreme Court. A 1999 decision of the U.S. Supreme Court narrowly upheld the rights of Minnesota and Wisconsin tribes to hunt, fish and gather in the territory ceded by the Treaty of 1837 (a broad area encompassing parts of the St. Croix River Valley and much of central Minnesota). That decision was begrudgingly accepted by Minnesota state government, where officials called for an end to the treaty rights fight, and for all citizens to acknowledge Indians' rights under treaties.

Environmental and Land Management Issues in Ojibwe Country

As tribes began the provision of services to their people under the self-determination policies and reasserted their treaty rights, they also became aware of the environmental issues affecting Ojibwe country. Tribal members from Bad River Reservation (Wisconsin) led a successful protest against the transport of hazardous chemicals across their reservations. Ojibwe tribes in northern Wisconsin, under the Great Lakes Fish and Wildlife Commission, have instituted ongoing fish toxicology studies of northern Wisconsin and Lake Superior waters, studies made necessary because of past environmental mismanagement from industry and mining. Similarly, Minnesota tribes have engaged in their own toxicology studies, as well as studies about the effects of acid rain on fishing and the wild rice crop.

Protester at the march on Lansing, Michigan, in 1995

Land management issues have also been the target of tribal interests. The Fond du Lac Band (Minnesota) led an effort to stop the development of the St. Louis River Valley, one of the few remaining wilderness valleys in the country and home to several wolf packs, eagles, and other protected species. Minnesota tribes have also led the effort to keep our elder brothers, the wolves, a protected species. Throughout Ojibwe country, tribes are acknowledging and accepting their unique responsibilities as guardians of the natural environment and protectors of our elder brothers.

A leading Ojibwe voice in both the treaty rights and environmental rights issues was the late Walt Bresette, a Red Cliff (Wisconsin) band member. Perhaps more than most contemporary Ojibwe people, Walt had both a regional and global perspective on our roles as guardians and treaty rights protectors, and recognized the importance of environmental protection in maintaining the global economy (Walter Bressette, 1998):

> So I think our rights, indigenous rights, treaty rights, will become a vital tool in the role in the restabilization of this economy. In addition I think the indigenous knowledge that we have with our elders will become a tool that will be used.

The Future

People like Walt Bresette epitomize an Ojibwe rekindling of the indigenous world view that people are the keepers of the natural world. This growing acknowledgment throughout Ojibwe country is shown in a variety of ways, including the careful management of resources on reservation and ceded lands, and the Ojibwe tribes' advocacy of environmental protection with state legislatures and the federal government.

There is acknowledgment among many indigenous people of the relationships and interrelationships of all things, and of the continuity of life into life forever. This profound sense of things has often been expressed in a circle, which represents the beginning and ending, the continuity of life, the nature of things, and their interrelationships. Perhaps this was best described by Black Elk, the great Oglala holy man (Neihardt, 1932, p. 194-196):

> Everything the Power of the World does is done in a circle. The sky is round, and I have heard the earth is round like a ball, and so are all the stars. The wind, in its greatest power, whirls. Birds make their nests in circles, for theirs is the same religion as ours. The sun comes forth and goes down again in a circle. The moon does the same, and both are round. Even the seasons form a great circle in their changing, and always come back again to where they were.

The Protect the Earth Eagle Feather Staff, with many special and sacred prayer bundles attached, arrives in the Capitol in 1998 after its historic 320 mile journey through the Ceded Territory to draw attention to the need to protect the air and water for the Seven Generations to come.

GIIWATAAWAYI'IJ
GAKINA GEGOO
WIIDOOKODAADIIMAGAD
BIMAADIZIWINING
(everything in the circle helps life)

"Everything the Power of the
World does is in a circle."
—Black Elk

The life of a man is a circle from childhood to childhood, so it is in everything where power moves. Our teepees were round like the nests of birds, and these were always set in a circle, the nation's hoop, a nest of many nests, where the Great Spirit meant for us to hatch our children.

Summary

AT THE BEGINNING OF THE CHAPTER, I told of taking my granddaughter and sons out to Wisconsin Point on the western end of Lake Superior, once a primary settlement for the early Ojibwe people of the area. Later I took them to St. Francis Cemetery in Superior to see the mass graves where our ancestors were moved. I have taken other people there as well; and I have taken them to other places, including the early Ojibwe settlement areas of Fond du Lac in West Duluth, and old village settlements near Perch Lake, Dead Fish Lake, and the old Fond du Lac village site on a hill overlooking the St. Louis River that flows through Nagahchiwanong (Fond du Lac Reservation). I have also taken groups to Madeline Island. I feel strongly that people should know the stories of these places, and that they should know of their responsibility in keeping these areas free from development, which would forever mask the great story of Ojibwe people. Our Ojibwe ancestors walk these and other sacred places, places worn with the paths of our great-grandparents and grandparents. Their physical beings have long ago been recycled into the very trees and grasses and birds and animals that now live on this earth. And that is what separates us from all the other people on this place we call Turtle Island. We have been here for many thousands of years. We are intricately interwoven into this place. We are part of the great circle of this place.

GIIKINOO'AMAADIWIN
We Gain Knowledge

Ways of Learning and Being: Education and Family Systems

In 1991 my reservation (Fond du Lac in northern Minnesota) received a small grant from the Minnesota Historical Society to send someone to Washington, D.C., to review the central office files of the Bureau of Indian Affairs for information about the reservation. I was that person. My month-long visit to the National Archives was a life-changing event, not just for me as an educator and historian, but also in a personal sense. It brought home to me the extent of the human tragedy that has come to define the federal government's role in the education of its indigenous people and the lingering effects on contemporary American Indian families and cultures. I was at the archives for three reasons: first, I was to collect microfiche, pictures, and photocopies of records of all things related to the Fond du Lac Reservation; second, a colleague (Dan Anderson) wanted me to gather information for him on the Bois Forte Reservation and Vermilion Boarding School near Tower, Minnesota; third, David Beaulieu (White Earth Ojibwe) asked me to look in the files of Genado Indian Boarding School for any information on the Beaulieu family.

The recollection of that visit is forever imbedded in my memory. The second file folder I opened contained a letter to the commissioner of Indian affairs. It was written by a mother requesting that she be allowed to keep her sons home from Pipestone Boarding School that year because she was ill and needed assistance in the home. I quickly went to the end of the letter and saw that it was signed by my great-grandmother and that her eldest son was my grandfather. A reply from the commissioner was attached, informing my great-grandmother that her sons must report to the boarding school as directed. Later, in reviewing other files, I found out that my great-grandmother died that winter in a flu epidemic that swept the reservation. I remember being overcome by a flood of emotions ranging from anger and disgust to grief. Anger and disgust for a government that believed it had the right to supervise the personal lives of the people whose nations it had possessed. Grief for a great-grandmother I had never known, someone who suddenly became more than just a tombstone in the old Catholic cemetery up the road from where I live, but a person to whom I felt a strong emotional connection.

Babies spent much of the first two years of their lives in a dikinagan (cradleboard), where they learned important life skills by observing and listening.

The impact of that powerful moment caused me to set down the file. My hands went to my face, and I wept quietly, causing discomfort to other researchers who were sitting near me. Their nervous coughs and sniffles echoed through the high spaces of that place. That incident brought history home to me. It put a human face on it for me and reminded me that we are both the products of and participants in history, that we are all part of a forever story that began in time immemorial and that continues beyond our own passing, to our children and their children.

There would be other moments when I brought discomfort to my neighboring research fellows. When I reviewed the files of the Genado Boarding School (Nebraska), I came upon the death files, which are the reports, telegrams, and memoranda that were sent to parents and their local Indian agents to inform them of the death of a child attending boarding school:

"We regretfully report that your son was found dead in a field . . ."

"We regretfully report that your daughter, along with two other girls, died after being hit by a train while on unauthorized [running away] leave from . . ."

There were hundreds, possibly thousands, of those types of letters.

That visit to our National Archives affected me as a historical researcher; I will forever refuse to distance myself abstractly from my research. My representation of the history of Ojibwe education will always contain some of my own story because I am Ojibwe. I am part of the story. Moreover, I am forever reminded of our indebtedness to our ancestors, grandparents, great-grandparents, and the people before them, who endured and survived a horrifying period of history so we could be here today, still proud of who we are, still strong in our ways.

Ojibwe children from their early years to around the age of seven were cared for and nurtured by grandmothers, aunties, and elders. This tradition continues today in our early childhood programs.

Letter written by Elizabeth Morrisette, author Tom Peacock's great-grandmother, August 19, 1916

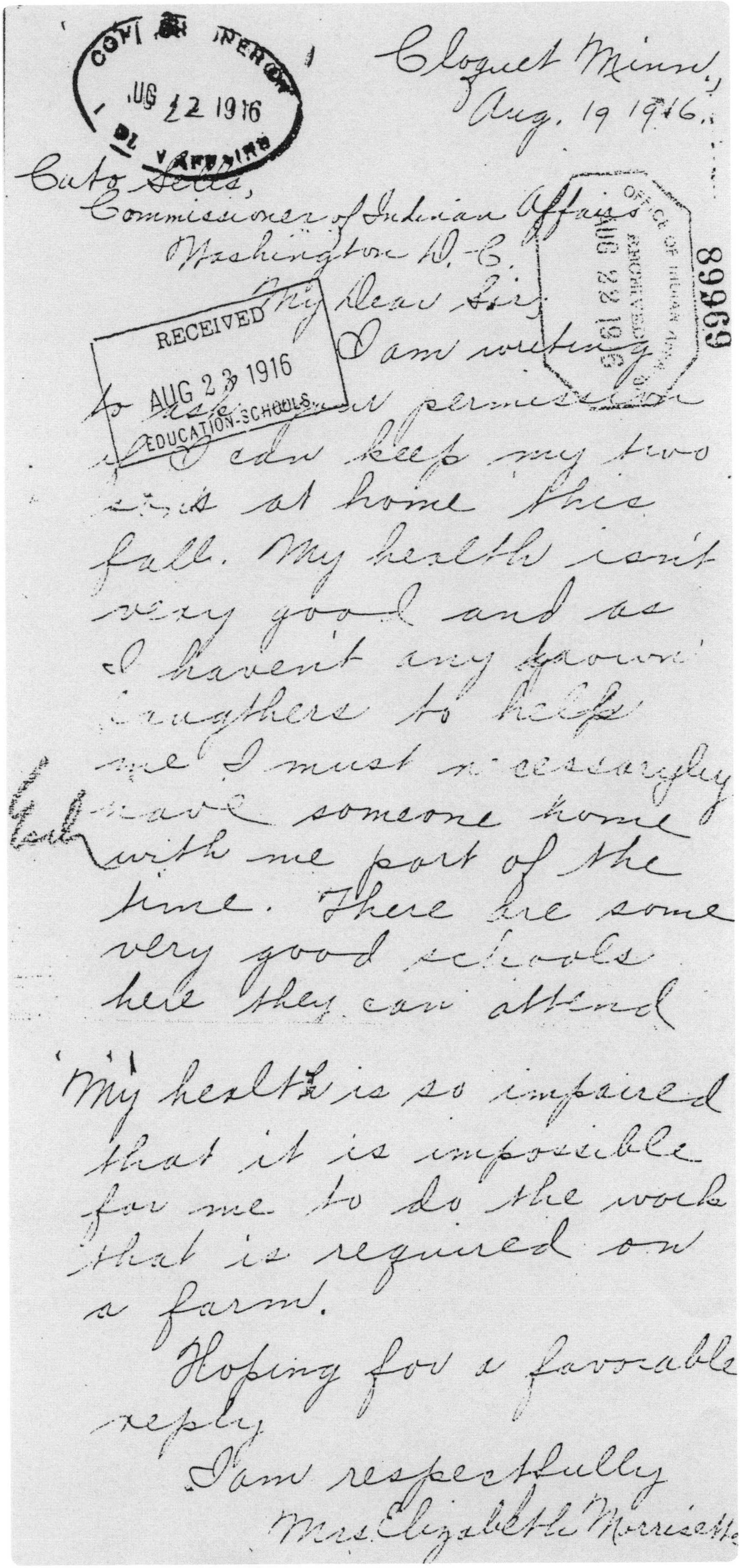

AUG 22 1916

RECEIVED
AUG 23 1916
EDUCATION-SCHOOLS

OFFICE OF INDIAN AFFAIRS
RECEIVED
AUG 22 1916

69668

Cloquet Minn,
Aug. 19 1916.

Cato Sells,
Commissioner of Indian Affairs
Washington D.C.

My Dear Sir,

I am writing to ask your permission if I can keep my two girls at home this fall. My health isn't very good and as I haven't any grown daughters to help me I must necessarily have someone home with me part of the time. There are some very good schools here they can attend

"My health is so impaired that it is impossible for me to do the work that is required on a farm.

Hoping for a favorable reply

I am respectfully
Mrs. Elizabeth Morrisette

GAGWE-WIIDOOKAAZOWAAD.
GEGO!
(They try to help. Don't!)

Ojibwe children learned from each other as they practiced skills they would use later in adult life.

A Chapter Road Map

THIS CHAPTER BEGINS WITH a description of traditional Ojibwe education (as it was before contact with Europeans), the path to wisdom, and traditional ways of teaching. The traditional Ojibwe family is described, including the clan and extended family system, as well as family roles and functions. The period of American assimilation, with all its components — Bureau of Indian Affairs, mission schools, government training schools, day schools, off-reservation boarding schools, on-reservation boarding schools, and the effects of formal education on the Ojibwe family — is described. There is a section on the American Indian education reform movement, including Indian citizenship, the Merriam Report, the movement of Ojibwe children to public schools, the effects of the Indian Reorganization Act on Indian education, the impact of the Elementary and Secondary Education Act, and the Kennedy Report on Indian Education. Contemporary Ojibwe education and families are discussed, including the period of self-determination, tribal schools, integration of Ojibwe language and culture into school curricula, a profile of an Ojibwe educational leader, tribal colleges, and an overview of the status of the Ojibwe family. Finally, we take a hopeful look toward the future, a time where we envision more tribally controlled schools, where we confront the issue of Ojibwe language loss, where decisions on schools and families are made at the local level, and where education moves to become learner-sensitive.

Traditional Ojibwe Education

The purposes of traditional Ojibwe education were both to serve the practical needs of the people (to learn life skills) and to enhance the soul (to grow in spiritual ways). Together they were part of the balance on one's journey on the path of life. To possess only the skills of living without knowledge of the spirit would be to live a life without purpose, depth, and meaning. To rely solely upon inner growth was to ignore the harsh reality of life in earlier times. Education of the traditional Ojibwe was in three phases (Johnston, 1976).

Until around the age of seven, children were cared for and nurtured by grandmothers, aunties, and elders. From about that age, young boys went with the men, fathers, uncles, and older cousins to learn the ways of men in providing sustenance by hunting and fishing. Centuries-old skills were passed down through the generations in this way. In the making of canoes, boys were taught how to take the bark from birch trees, how to shape the gunwales, ribs, and flooring of green cedar saplings, how to harvest and split the roots of spruce that would be used for threading, how to collect and mix spruce resin with grease and the black powder of cedar, and how to measure the canoe's dimensions using their own human dimensions. More importantly, at an early age they were taught how to make the bow and arrows used in hunting. With a boy's first kill, the whole village would celebrate, and the kill would be the main part of the feast.

Girls remained with their grandmothers and aunties to learn the ways of women, to raise crops, to gather plants for food, and to provide for the home in other ways. For example, they were taught to make the nets used in fishing, how to gather the basswood or nettle cord, how to dry it, how to separate the fibers by wetting them and drawing them through their mouths, how to roll the fibers, and how to tie the netting fiber in different patterns for catching different kinds of fish. Girls were also taught to tan animal hides, how to remove the flesh, wash off the bloodstains, soak the hide, scrape off the hair, soak it in deer brains, scrape the hide again, then stretch it on a frame.

The third phase of education was when people began a search for wisdom. This search would consume the rest of an individual's life: a quest to know the whole story of things, to know things in their simplicity and in their complexity, to know the many layers of meaning. Wisdom is the whole of these things (Johnston, 1976, p. 70):

Ojibwe women and girls, 1900. In traditional times, girls remained with their grandmothers and aunties to learn the ways of women, to raise crops, to gather plants for sustenance, and to provide for the home in other ways.

It was during this final stage in life that the learner realized his want of knowledge, and sought out the wise to teach him. A man or woman begins to learn, when he seeks out knowledge and wisdom; wisdom will not seek him. He may never attain it, but he can live by those principles given to him.

Teaching the Path of Life

The individual journey in search of wisdom led people to try to live their lives in ways that would bring honor to both themselves and to all those whose lives they touched. Just like contemporary Ojibwe, our ancestors were human and their will was sometimes weak, and just like us, living the good way was often the most difficult lesson to learn and to integrate into their daily living. Their pathway on how to live the gentle way, just like ours, is through prayer and fasting, through listening to everything for its deeper meaning, through observing all the subtlety and nuances of life, and through learning the whole story of things. The path was taught as part of the spiritual teachings of the Midewiwin (the Ojibwe religion) as a way to ensure that when a person's soul passed into the spirit world he or she would be guaranteed a place in the Land of Souls (Johnston, 1982). The path was one of gentleness, humbleness, and respect (Johnston, 1982):

— Honor Gitchi Manito (the Great Mystery, the Creator).

— Honor elders. Honor your grandmothers and grandfathers, parents, aunties and uncles, and all elders we encounter. Someday if we live our lives in such a way, we too will be so honored.

— Honor our elder brothers (all the animals are considered our elder brothers as they were here before us, and we rely on them in our teachings, as well as for sustenance).

— Honor women. Honor our grandmothers and mothers, aunties, sisters and wives, our weedjiwagan (our partners in the path of life).

— Keep our promises and uphold our pledges.

— Kindness should be shown to everyone, even those with whom we disagree. This can be difficult, but is necessary if we are to live in a way which will honor ourselves and all others.

— Be peaceful in body and spirit.

— Be courageous.

— Be moderate in our dreams, thoughts, words, and deeds.

The teachings to attain wisdom were all around our ancestors as they are also all around us as contemporary Ojibwe. From their elders and spiritual people, our ancestors learned the values and spiritual lessons that would guide their lives. From their elder brothers, the

Boys playing mocassin game

Moccasin game, White Earth, 1920. From about the age of seven, young boys learned the ways of men from fathers, uncles, and older cousins.

animals, they learned lessons of gentleness, courage, and keenness of vision. From silence, they gained the knowledge to contemplate and to think through things before acting. From the wind and lapping of water and from birds, they learned the beauty and depth of music. These same things are still with us today. We need only to listen and to observe things to perceive their deeper meaning. Moreover, just as with our ancestors, the path to wisdom really comes down to simple things, simple yet complex at the same time: honor the Creator, honor elders, be kind, be peaceful. Live in a gentle way.

Ways of teaching

Babies spent much of the first two years of their lives in a dikinagan (cradleboard), where they learned the important life skills of observation and listening. As their parents worked outside, little Ojibwe children would watch the dance of life around them — the play of light and shadow, the movement of grasses, the sparkle of sun through branches, and the habits of people and animals. As young children, they honed their skill of observation. This traditional attribute served the Ojibwe well as hunters and gatherers, as warriors, and as keen observers of the subtlety and nuances of both human and animal behavior. Moreover, as the young witnessed the goings on of life from their dikinagan, they also learned the art of listening. All around them were the sounds of life: the chatter of squirrels, the whisper of grasses, the songs of wind through trees, and the inflection of voice in their parents, grandmothers and grandfathers, and aunties. The art of listening was further refined into adulthood, as they sought out others for wisdom, as they sought out the deeper meaning of things, and as they sought out all the layers of stories. Listening and observation are skills still prized throughout contemporary Ojibwe country and

acknowledged by many non-Indians, who often remark on these abilities.

While growing up, the young were taught the history and ways of the people, as well as many of the lessons of life, by the parables, fables, allegories, songs, chants, and dances of their elders, grandmothers, and grandfathers (Johnston, 1976). Because young children are filled with questions, stories, often humorous in nature, were used as a way to explain the why of things. If children were to ask why there were seasons, a story would be told, which explained the struggle between the spirits of winter and summer. If they were to ask why birch trees have black marks, a story would follow about when Waynabozho (the cultural hero and great teacher of the Ojibwe) was teasing the thunderbirds, and the thunderbirds threw down great bolts of lightening at Waynabozho but hit birch trees instead. If children asked why ducks walk the way they do, a story would be used to inform them about the ways and whys of ducks. This storytelling tradition was described by George Copway (in Hilger, 1992, p. 58):

Legends are of three distinct classes, namely, the amusing, the historical, and the moral. In the fall we have one class, in the winter another, and in the spring a third. . . .

Some of these stories are most exciting, and so intensely interesting, that I have seen children during their relation, whose tears would flow quite plentifully, and their breasts heave with thoughts too big for utterance.

Night after night for weeks have I sat and eagerly listened to these stories. The days following, the characters would haunt me at every step, and every moving leaf would seem to be a voice of a spirit. To those days I look back with pleasurable emotions.

Our ancestors' stories were filled with both obvious, simple teachings and deeper, more subtle meanings. Values such as not being greedy, giving to others, and being kind and respectful were the kinds of deeper meanings in stories. In a sense, these stories had messages for all, both children and adults alike. Moreover, the deeper meanings of stories were seldom directly conveyed. It was up to the listeners, who would go away from storytelling thinking about their meanings, to try to figure out the messages on their own. This subtle, indirect way of teaching remains an important cultural way among the Ojibwe today. Sometimes we are given advice without recognizing it as such. If we have done something that can be interpreted as being greedy, someone may tell us a story of a person who was greedy or a story about a time he was greedy. If we have caused harm through hurtful words, someone may recall a time he hurt another with his words. The teachings are always indirect. The storytelling tradition, as a way of conveying historical and cultural knowledge, has survived colonization and continues today (Broker, 1983, p. 3):

Now my children are urging me to recall all the stories and bits of information that I ever heard my grandparents or any of the older Ojibway tell. It is important, they say, because now their children are asking them. Others are saying the same thing. It is well that they are asking, for the Ojibway young must learn their cycle.

In traditional times, when the young were nearing adolescence, boys needed to seek a vision, but girls could also go on a vision quest

When the young were nearing adolescence, boys needed to seek a vision, but girls could also go on a vision quest if they wished. Generally, they were brought by their fathers to a place where they would seek visions. Always this was a place conducive to thought and to dreams.

if they wished. It was felt that females, because they have the ability to create life itself, were born fulfilled. Just like the Creator, whose vision led to the creation of the earth, stars, and all of life, men needed vision in order to find their purpose in life. Seeking a vision required that one try to live out the meaning of the vision.

The first step was to receive an Ojibwe name. Young people were given their names by elders, usually grandfathers or grandmothers, but especially those elders who were not ill. The giving of a name was important for several reasons. If a child died before receiving a name, the child's spirit would not be able to enter the Land of Souls. Furthermore, the spirits could not communicate with people without first addressing them by their Ojibwe names.

Chippewa Indians on the shore of Cass Lake near Walker, Minnesota, ca. 1900

Before going on their vision quests, boys would first be brought into the sweat lodge for purification. Here, both their bodies and spirits would be cleansed by the vapors and the prayer. Next they were brought, generally by their fathers, to a place where they would seek their visions. Always this was a place conducive to thought and dreams. In a specially constructed shelter built by their fathers, they would remain for a period of up to four days, not eating and only rarely taking a drink. Here they would eventually experience their vision. Sometimes it was necessary to fast several times in order to attain a vision or to seek the deeper meanings of a vision. The dream was not shared with others; to do so was to give up one's inner soul (Johnston, 1976, p. 127):

But when it did come [the vision], it was regarded as personal not to be disclosed to others; nor were others to interfere with the vision or the quest of another person. It was said, "Do not give away your soul-spirit; Do not attempt to enter the soul-spirit of another." To reveal one's spirit was tantamount to surrender of self and a loss of freedom. An attempt to enter the inner being of another person was construed as an act of possession.

In addition to using observation, listening, stories, and vision quests as teaching ways, gifting was also used. In traditional times when one wanted to know something, the person would approach someone of knowledge with a gift of tobacco and a prized personal possession. Acceptance of the gifts was an acknowledgment that the individual would try to answer the questions of the one seeking knowledge. This manner of conveying knowledge, of looking for the deeper meanings and interpretation of dreams and life events and of answers to questions that trouble people, is still used in contemporary Ojibwe communities. Whenever advice or knowledge is sought from elders and others of experience, tobacco and a gift, often a blanket, are still used.

The Traditional Ojibwe Family

In a metaphysical sense, some Ojibwe would define the Anishinabe (Ojibwe) as all people and the elder brothers (all animals), as well as the plants. This broad definition of family recognizes the relationships and interrelationships of all living things of the earth and is an acknowledgment of the earth as mother of all things. In some respects, this is similar to the Lakota belief, "Mitakuye Oyasin" (we are all related). Others might define their Ojibwe family to include the larger family of people related to the Ojibwe; this would encompass those tribes who share aspects of culture, history, and language. Using that definition, tribes such as the Ottawa, Pottawatomi, Menominee, Penobscot, Passamaquaddy, Wampanoag, Blackfeet, Yurok, Wiyot, Cree, Shawnee, Cheyenne, and others are part of the greater family. All of us have the Lenape (Delaware) ancestry in common.

Within the traditional Ojibwe family, however, the first delineation of kinship was the dodaim (which some refer to as "totem"), or clan system. "Waenaesh k'dodaem?" (What is your dodaim?) is still asked among Ojibwe people. The origin of the dodaim is said to have occurred when the Ojibwe lived on the eastern ocean, and six beings emerged from the sea. One being returned to the sea after harsh exposure to the light and heat of the sun. The other five came to shore and lived among the Ojibwe.

Dodaim membership in the Ojibwe descended through the father's line (Warren, 1984), and marriage within the same dodaim was not allowed. The system was described by Warren (1984, p. 45):

Dodaim (clan) symbols

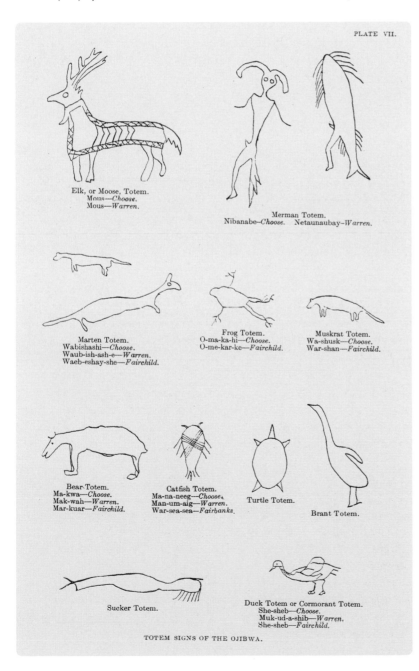

PLATE VII.

Elk, or Moose, Totem.
Mons—*Choose.*
Mous—*Warren.*

Merman Totem.
Nibanabe—*Choose.* Netaunaubay—*Warren.*

Marten Totem.
Wabishashi—*Choose.*
Waub-ish-ash-e—*Warren.*
Waeb-eshay-she—*Fairchild.*

Frog Totem.
O-ma-ka-hi—*Choose.*
O-me-kar-ke—*Fairchild.*

Muskrat Totem.
Wa-shusk—*Choose.*
War-shan—*Fairchild.*

Bear Totem.
Ma-kwa—*Choose.*
Mak-wah—*Warren.*
Mar-kuar—*Fairchild.*

Catfish Totem.
Ma-na-neeg—*Choose.*
Man-um-aig—*Warren.*
War-sea-sea—*Fairbanks.*

Turtle Totem.

Brant Totem.

Sucker Totem.

Duck Totem or Cormorant Totem.
She-sheb—*Choose.*
Muk-ud-a-shib—*Warren,*
She-sheb—*Fairchild.*

TOTEM SIGNS OF THE OJIBWA.

The crane [chejauk], catfish [mizi], bear [noka], marten [waubizhaezh], wolf [myeengun], and loon [mong], are the principal families, not only in the civil point of view, but in numbers, as they comprise eight-tenths of the whole tribe. Many of these Totems are not known to the tribe in general, and the writer has learned them only through close inquiry. Among these may be named the goose, beaver, sucker, sturgeon, gull, hawk, cormorant, and the whitefish totems.

Johnston (1976) explained the dodaim as serving particular functions in traditional Ojibwe society: leadership (chiefs), defense (warriors), sustenance (hunters), learning (teachers), and medicine (healers). From these five principal dodaim, others were added (Johnston, 1976):

1. Leadership — crane, goose, loon, hawk, sparrow hawk, white headed eagle, black headed eagle, brant, seagull

2. Defense — bear, wolf, lynx

3. Sustenance — marten, beaver, moose, caribou, deer, muskrat

4. Learning — catfish, pike, sucker, sturgeon, whitefish

5. Medicine — turtle, otter, rattlesnake, black snake, frog, merman or mermaid.

Courting photo taken in 1875

Family Structure

In traditional Ojibwe society, when a young man became interested in a young woman, he would court her. This could take the form of visits (where the girl's parents or grandparents were always present). Sometimes he would play a love flute (made with cedar or sumac) near her. If his intentions were serious, he would kill game and deliver it to the girl's family to show that he was capable of being a good provider. Courting couples were not allowed, however, to be alone together (Hilger, 1992). Girls, in particular, were often in the close company of their mothers, aunties, and grandmothers.

Many marriages were arranged. The marriage ceremony itself usually involved the boy simply moving into the wigiwam (wigwam) of the girl's parents for a period of a year, after which the young couple would move out to establish their own home. In the Ojibwe language, one's husband or wife is referred to as weedjiwagan, a partner in the path of life. An arranged marriage was described by a Lac Courte Oreille man to Hilger (1992, p. 159):

My first wife died. She was a good woman; I admired her. I went to her uncle (her parents were dead) and asked for her sister. I gave many things to her uncle: quilts that I have received in dances, as well as food. The girl's brother asked her nicely to marry me, and so she did. There was no marriage ceremony.

Children were considered a special gift from the Creator, and their arrival was celebrated with a feast. Their dried naval cords were saved in hopes that the cord would help a child on the path toward wisdom. It was put in a leather pouch and hung over the dikinagan until the child was a year old or more (Hilger, 1992, pp. 16-17):

In the old days on the Lac Courte Oreille Reservation, after a boy was a year old, his naval bag was placed in the stump of an old tree and ashes were thrown over it in the hope that a bear might find it and thereby make a lucky hunter of the boy. A girl's cord was buried under wood chips in order that she might become a diligent wood gatherer.

"I placed my little boy's in the trunk of a tree. This is done all around here today," said one mother on the same reservation.

Extended families were part of the social structure of traditional Ojibwe communities. Grandparents, aunties, uncles, cousins, brothers, and sisters were all considered close family, unlike contemporary Euro-American families in which only the father, mother, and children constitute the family. Moreover, family members had particular roles to fulfill. Paternal uncles were often the disciplinarians of young boys. If a boy needed to have a conversation with an adult about some aspect of their manners or behavior, it was often the uncles who called them away for a talk. For their part, grandparents and aunties played important parts as care givers and disciplinarians. In a general sense, the community shared responsibility for the raising of the young. Aunties, grandparents, and neighbors would all take responsibility for talking to children, giving them "the look," or making a clucking sound (which signified that the child was being naughty and had better behave).

Ojibwe education made an abrupt transition in the nineteenth century from learning the old ways to the formal schooling mandated by the government and churches.

The Period of Early Contact and American Colonization

The coming of Europeans to North America touched nearly every aspect of Ojibwe culture — language, ways of being and knowing, values, spiritual ways, and family, social, institutional, and governmental structures. The People (Ojibwe) still suffer from the effects of that period of history, from all of its undeniable oppression and its accompanying depression and dysfunction. The dysfunction manifests itself in high student drop-out rates and low academic achievement, a mistrust of formal schooling, high rates of adolescent pregnancy, poverty, and high rates of crime in Indian country (Cleary and Peacock, 1998). In some Ojibwe communities, there remains a lingering bitterness and resentment toward Euro-American culture. There is no denying that the taking of our homelands marked the beginnings of many of today's social ills among the Ojibwe. The oral history of our people has no mention of any of these societal ills before colonization.

What we do know is that during the period of colonization the indigenous population of North America was reduced by disease, war, slavery, and dislocation from ten million to fewer than one million (Zinn, 1980). Whole tribes that had flourished for many thousands of years were eliminated. Whole cultures, perhaps speaking as many as two thousand languages and prospering with sophisticated culture and technology, were wiped from the face of the earth in the name of manifest destiny (Zinn, 1980, p. 16):

Boys' and girls' classes at the Ojibwe School at Lac du Flambeau in the 1800s. Schools for Ojibwe children had a regimented, military style.

Behind the English invasion of North America, behind their massacre of Indians, their deception, their brutality, was that special powerful drive in civilizations based on private property. It was a morally ambiguous drive; the need for space, for land, was a real human need. But in conditions of scarcity, in a barbarous epoch of history ruled by competition, this human need was transformed into the murder of whole peoples.

The devastation of that historical period affected not only our Lenape relatives (Zinn recalled an example of the Wampanoag of Martha's Vineyard who were reduced from three thousand to just over three hundred souls by 1764), but affected the Ojibwe as well. Smallpox and flu epidemics claimed nearly half the residents of the Fond du Lac Reservation (Minnesota) in the early twentieth century, a situation repeated in many Ojibwe communities from Michigan to North Dakota. For the survivors, their "civilization and Christianization" began. The official governmental policy of denying American Indians their languages and cultures and assimilating them into American society began in 1617, when King James ordered the building of schools and churches for the "education of ye children of these Barbarians in Virginia" (Reyhner and Eder, 1992), and continued well into the 1960s.

With the early French traders came the Jesuit and Franciscan missionaries. It was their mission to convert people they believed were pagan, devoid of any knowledge of God, to Christianity. Like other missionaries in other parts of the world, their first step in doing this was to learn the language. One of the these early missionaries, Father Frederic Baraga, developed an Ojibwe dictionary. Bibles were followed by hymn books, which were followed by primers.

Formal Education in Ojibwe Country

The formal education of Ojibwe young initially took place in immigrant homes and churches. Many of the first formally educated Ojibwe were the mixed-blood children from Ojibwe and French intermarriage. Soon, however, mission churches and schools were opened in Ojibwe communities, including Red Cliff, Odana, Red Lake, Fond du Lac, Bellcourt, and others. At first these schools were operated by Christian missionaries; later they were paid for by the federal government (Vizenor, 1987, p. 128):

Sherman Hall, the superintendent of the school at La Pointe (Madeline Island, Wisconsin), wrote a letter to a government agent that the teachers have continued

Lac du Flambeau Indian School Band. Indian students in boarding schools were introduced to non-traditional activities such as playing in a band.

"their labors as usual, endeavoring to instruct all who were willing to receive instruction from us, in the duties and doctrines of the Christian religion, and in letters. . . .

The school during the year numbered sixty-five different scholars, forty-three males, and twenty-two females. It has been kept in operation regularly during the year, except the usual vacations. . . . The proficiency of the scholars who have been regular attendants is very satisfactory. The branches taught have been spelling, reading, writing, arithmetic, geography, and composition.

The federal role in Indian education grew markedly with the passage of the Indian Civilization Act of 1824, which provided federal funding for the formal schooling of Indians. Mission schools were soon complemented by federal manual (trade) and boarding schools. By 1838 the federal government was operating six manual and 87 boarding schools for American Indian students (Reyhner and Eder, 1992). Later, Ojibwe young people were sent to off-reservation boarding schools located in Pipestone, Minnesota; Flandreau, South Dakota; and Carlisle, Pennsylvania; and to on-reservation boarding schools like the mission school in Odana, Wisconsin. The stories of Ojibwe people who attended these schools are just beginning to be written. In *Red World and White* (1973), John Rogers eloquently captured memoirs of his boarding school days at Flandreau Indian School. Pigskin Peterson (Grand Portage) told of his schooling at Carlisle Indian School (Pennsylvania), after which he returned to the reservation as an accomplished fiddler. Betty Gurno (Fond du Lac) recalled her boarding school experiences at Flandreau Indian School in *A Long Time Ago Is Just Like Today* (1976) and *A Forever Story: The People and Community of the Fond du Lac Reservation* (Peacock, 1998). Her experiences of being punished for speaking Ojibwe and not being allowed to learn anything of her Ojibwe culture and heritage are forever burned into her memory. Frank and Joe Martineau told of nuns at the mission school in Odana, Wisconsin, who intercepted their mother's care packages, cut the boys' socks in half, wore the bottoms of the socks, and forced the boys to wear only the socks' tops (so it looked as though they had on socks). Linda Grover's (Grand Portage) creative interpretation of the effects of boarding

Many Indian children died of loneliness, disease, and abuse in boarding schools or while attempting to run away.

The number of children attending boarding schools and the regimentation of the schools is reflected in this undated Mt. Pleasant, Michigan, school picture.

schools on both the past and current generation of Ojibwe is filled with gut-wrenching, heart-breaking episodes of homesickness, abuse, and brainwashing to reject one's cultural heritage (Grover, 1999). Elizabeth Albert (*A Forever Story*) expressed the irony she felt when she worked as Head Start director in Red Cliff, Wisconsin, and tried to instill cultural pride in children at the same mission school her father had attended up through the eighth grade under the stern tutelage of nuns who taught him nothing of his history or language or culture.

The effects of mission and boarding schools on Ojibwe people were many. Young people who were sent to these schools often did not return home during the entire school year. Mothers and fathers were not able to parent their children and soon lost the ability to parent. A particular institutionalized behavior resulted from boarding school education, and some of these young people grew into adults who did not know how to parent children. Loss of culture resulted, with the young losing their link to the elders and to the vast store-house of traditional knowledge. Many young people lacked the ability to communicate with elders and other traditional people in the Ojibwe language, so elders were no longer looked to for their knowledge and wisdom. The systematic policy of using education to remove the Ojibwe culture from young Ojibwe people, coupled with the banning of religious practices, resulted in the loss of language, the loss of parenting skills, and the low self-esteem in several generations of Indian people. These remain issues in Ojibwe country today, where drop-out rates of students hover near 40 percent (Quality Education for Minorities Project, 1990).

The Period of American Indian Education Reform

The erosion of tribal cultures through the forced assimilation policies of the federal government had a devastating effect on American Indian people, who had also relinquished 140 million acres of land in the process (Gilliland, 1988). Ojibwe tribes had given up most of the states of Wisconsin, northern Michigan, and Minnesota, and were confined to small

St. Mary's School (Red Lake)
basketball team, 1951

reservation areas, many of which were on marginal lands unfit for agriculture or other purposes. There are many stories of the helplessness and poverty throughout Ojibwe country during the period of federal dependency, of influenza outbreaks, of starvation resulting from rations being late, and of the forced displacement of people, as villages were relocated and people dispersed onto their allotments. This was a time of great national suffering for Ojibwe people. Yet, it also showed the People's tenacity and will to survive despite all odds. The fact that Ojibwe ways endured through this difficult period is a testament to our ancestors.

With a national movement for social change in the early 1920s, some efforts were made to reverse federal policy toward Indians. All American Indians who had not been declared "competent" (the government had a process whereby Indians could be declared "competent" and earn citizenship) became citizens under the Indian Citizenship Act of 1924. The Merriam Report of 1928 was a scathing rebuke of federal assimilation policies. It cited the intense poverty and destitution in Indian country and the loss of

Ponemah Indian School (Red Lake Nation), 1940. Nursery schools were established during and soon after the Depression as a way to employ teachers and to feed and teach children.

tribal cultures and languages, and it called for reform in the federal government's efforts in Indian country (Gilliland, 1988). Under the leadership of John Collier, commissioner of Indian affairs in the 1930s and 1940s, the teaching of tribal cultures and languages was encouraged in schools. Policies were adopted to discourage the attendance of elementary-age children in boarding schools and to develop more day schools in Indian communities. In addition, with the passage of the Johnson-O'Malley Act of 1934, the federal government supplemented state public schools, thereby encouraging them to accept more Indian students (Reyhner and Eger, 1992). The Indian Reorganization Act of 1934 led to the development of the modern tribal governments that would become a strong voice for Indian education reform in local communities.

The effects of these reforms appeared in Ojibwe country. Former federal day schools became state public schools, such as the schools in Grand Portage, Nett Lake, and other Ojibwe communities. Fewer Ojibwe students attended off-reservation boarding schools, and the majority began to be educated at local public schools, including Hayward, Wisconsin; L'anse, Michigan; Sault Ste. Marie, Michigan; and Cass Lake, Minnesota.

This period of reform was short-lived because the Great Depression dried up the funding needed to make necessary changes. During the 1940s and 1950s, the country returned to the policy of assimilation. The teaching of Indian culture and languages was again discouraged in schools, and federal teachers no longer were provided summer institutes or other training for teaching Indian students.

Self-determination through Education

The 1960s were a tumultuous period in American history, especially regarding issues of civil rights, and this had a profound effect on American Indians. What began with the landmark civil rights case, Brown vs. Board of Education of Topeka in 1954 (347 U.S. 483), which declared that separate schools for minorities were not legal, evolved into the civil rights demonstrations and urban riots of the 1960s. The civil rights of all oppressed groups, including American Indians, appeared on the public policy agenda. This eventually led to a fundamental shift in federal policy when, in 1970, President Richard Nixon declared (Reyhner and Eger, 1992, p. 54):

It is long past that the Indian policies of the Federal government began to recognize and build upon the capacities and insights of the Indian people. Both as a matter of justice and as a matter of enlightened social policy, we must begin to act on the basis of what the Indians themselves have long been telling us. The time has come to break decisively with the past and to create the conditions for a new era in which the Indian future is determined by Indian acts and Indian decisions.

The period of self-determination of American Indians began with Nixon's speech and eventually led to a host of federal legislation designed to allow American Indian tribes to have more say in their own well-being. Already, the Elementary and Secondary Education Act (ESEA) of 1965 was having some positive effects on Indian education, as supplemental reading and mathematics programs began to be available to Indian students in both public and federal schools. Conditions for American Indian students, however, were deplorable by any standard, and these were reported in

NE YĀĀ SHIING GIKINOO 'IMĀĀGANĀG

(students of Mille Lacs village)

Students at Mille Lacs Vineland, 1925

GITIGE GIKENDAASOWIN
ANOKII WIN
(farm knowledge, work).

Attempts were made to turn Ojibwe people into farmers. Boarding school students performed farm chores on school-run farms, such as this one at St. Mary's mission.

two national Indian education studies, beginning with the National Study of American Indian Education (summarized in *To Live on This Earth*, Fuchs and Havighurst, 1972). The second study was done by the Special Senate Subcommittee on Indian Education and was published as *Indian Education: A National Tragedy, a National Challenge* (U.S. Senate, 1969). Known as the Kennedy Report, the study led to passage of the Indian Education Act of 1972 (Reyhner and Eger, 1992). Title IV, as it came to be known, provided funding for the development of special programs for Indian students in schools. Many issues, however, remained (Grover, 1999):

The Class of 1968
Ten little, nine little, eight little Indians,
seven little, six little, five little Indians,
four little, three little, two little Indians
one little Indian . . .
And that left me, the last one
of the bunch, kindergartners of 1955
our teachers, the shade of our skin, our histories
those random chances silent banshees chasing children
one by one out of our parent's dreams, til I was
the only one left, and the one perceived as leaving,
leaving Vicky, pregnant in the 8th grade, who never came back
Vernon and George, nomads between res and town til they were forgotten
Wanda, always sick and agonizingly shy, who disappeared
Birdeen, who went to work after her father died
Percy and John, expelled for fighting
Susan, for skipping school to take care of the younger kids at home
Jim, who studied incorrigibility at juvenile hall
Pete, who perfected that art at Red Wing
Eliza, who never learned to read, and waited for sixteenth birthday
Bonita, who almost made it but "had to" get married, as we said in 1968
and that left me, the last one
the forgotten the untouched the protected
the bookish the lucky the lonely
the pride of her family
the last one.

During the 1960s, family issues also came to the forefront in Ojibwe country. Prior to the passage of the Indian Child Welfare Act (ICWA), many Ojibwe children were placed in non-Indian foster and adoptive homes, often far from their reservation communities. This was another tragic outgrowth of assimilation policy. Tribal governments and their social service agencies had little if any say in these placements, as foster care and adoption were under the jurisdiction of counties and states. Whole families were broken up, and stories abound throughout Ojibwe country of children who grew up being bounced from foster home to foster home, rarely or never getting to visit their parents and family back on the reservation and not getting to know anything of their background and heritage. That began to change with the passage of the ICWA as tribal governments developed their own child welfare advocate offices, began licensing on-reservation Indian foster homes, and began placing Ojibwe children who were in need of adoption in Ojibwe adoptive homes.

Contemporary Ojibwe Education and Families

The 1960s had seen a resurgence in ethnic pride, and in Ojibwe country there was both a cultural and spiritual awakening. As more Indian people went into higher education, Indian studies departments were developed in colleges and universities with significant American Indian student populations. With the enactment of the Indian Education Act (IEA) of 1972 and the funding appropriated for its implementation, a new cadre of American Indian school employees entered the public schools as home-school coordinators, Indian youth advocates, social worker aides, language and culture teachers, and tutors. For the first time in many schools, Indian students had an adult, many times an Indian person, to act as an advocate and represent them in school matters. Indian clubs were formed in many schools with significant Indian enrollment, and efforts were made to add Ojibwe culture, language, and history to the curriculum of some schools. Perhaps most importantly, the IEA empowered Indian parents by mandating American Indian parent committees in all schools having Indian education programs.

This new attention to the educational conditions of American Indians in public schools sometimes led to conflict between Ojibwe communities and nearby public schools. Many Ojibwe students continued to score lower than their non-Indian peers on standardized achievement tests, had higher drop-out rates, were more likely to be referred for special educational services, and were more often targeted for both in-school and out-of-school suspension. American Indian parent committees sometimes demanded changes in the ways schools provided education to their Indian students, requesting that districts hire American Indian teachers and administrators. Parent committees also sought representation on local school boards and pushed for a curriculum that was inclusive of Ojibwe culture and history. Frustrated with the unwillingness or inability of local school officials to respond to their demands, some parents pulled their children out of school and set up all-Indian schools. Indian student walk-outs at Cass Lake, Minnesota, led the Leech Lake Reservation to begin a small store-front school for Indian students, just across the street from Cass Lake High School. What began with little funding and few books is now Bugonaygeshing

AGINDAASOOWIGAMIGOON
(at the library)

By the 1940s and 1950s, many Ojibwe children were beginning to attend area public schools. This Ojibwe girl is using the library in a Cass Lake school (Leech Lake), 1952.

School, one of the largest primarily all-Indian schools in Ojibwe country. Similarly, Indian parents in the Onamia School District of Minnesota set up their own school on the Mille Lacs Reservation.

Some of these new schools were initially funded with IEA funds, while others soon obtained more permanent operational funding from the Bureau of Indian Affairs, Office of Indian Education Programs. Urban schools like the Heart of the Earth Survival School in Minneapolis and Red School House in St. Paul (now closed) began under the leadership of urban Indian parents and the American Indian Movement (AIM). Tribal schools, operating under the auspices of local tribal governments, were founded at Lac Courte Oreilles Reservation (LCO Ojibwa School), Cass Lake (Bugoneygeshing School), White Earth (Circle of Life School), Mille Lacs (Nay Ah Shing School), and Fond du Lac (Fond du Lac Ojibway School). These schools combine both traditional academics and a solid core of Ojibwe curriculum.

David Beaulieu

The growth in Indian education programs was led by new and dynamic leaders in Indian education. One such leader was David Beaulieu (White Earth), who emerged as a leader in the Indian education movement in Minnesota. He soon became a national Indian education leader when he was selected as the director of Indian education, U.S. Office of Education, where he serves as a voice for Indian education throughout the country (Beaulieu, 1998):

The new feature in Indian education is the institutionalization of education for Indians under Indian control, and that process has been an amazing process of transformation, and of rediscovery. That movement has been as exciting at the same time as it's been filled with deceit [the boarding school movement] and false starts.

Ojibwe protesters at the Michigan capitol in Lansing were seeking a better education for their children, 1995.

ALONG WITH THE DEVELOPMENT of Indian education programs in public schools and the tribally operated schools and Indian studies departments in colleges and universities also came the formation of tribal colleges. Tribal colleges serve a unique function in their communities, providing regular two-year transfer programs, certificate programs that allow graduates to enter the work force after two years, and a host of Ojibwe cultural and language offerings. More importantly, they provide the kind of support many Indian students need to make it in higher education — local, small, personalized student services and financial aid, Indian faculty and administration, and a focus on serving the local community. In Ojibwe country, one of the first tribal colleges was at Turtle Mountain, North Dakota. In Wisconsin, Lac Court Oreilles Ojibwa Community College began operations. Soon thereafter, Fond du Lac Tribal and Community College opened its doors under the leadership of President L. Jack Briggs, a Fond du Lac enrollee. Leech Lake Tribal College began under the leadership of one of their own, President Larry P. Aitken.

Both Aitken and Briggs are home-grown products of their respective reservations, educated in area colleges and universities only to return home to create tribal higher education institutions. More

Jaime Sam, student at Nay-Ah-Shing School (Mille Lacs), 1995. Some Ojibwe communities have established their own tribally operated schools.

recently, White Earth Reservation Tribal College began providing a locally based community college under the leadership of President Helen Klassen, a White Earth enrollee.

The important ingredients in all of these recent developments is that Ojibwe people have gained some control of the educational decision-making process, and the result is that Indian people have more and better choices. American Indian students from pre-school through post-secondary school have a range of options, including local Head Start programs and public, private, parochial, or tribally operated schools, as well as area community colleges, four-year colleges and universities, or tribal colleges.

Status of the Ojibwe Family

Just as progress has been made in the area of education, so also has the status of the Ojibwe family improved. Jobs created both by the development of tribal infrastructures (tribal governments) and the host of programs they offer to serve the population and, more recently, by gaming, have generated a more promising economic future where there was little hope several decades ago. These jobs have opened the door for choices, improved self-confidence, a better standard of living, and the move from dependence to independence. However, for many families and communities throughout the country, regardless of race or background, troubling issues remain (Cleary and Peacock, 1998): substance abuse (alcohol, drugs), all the present-day manifestations of oppression (institutional racism, overt and covert racism), malfunctioning institutions, and communities in trouble (alcoholism, drug abuse, poverty, crime, racism, class conflict).

What has changed is our collective consciousness, our sense that we have the solutions to these issues and that these solutions lie in the strength and tenacity of our culture. One of the tenants of our cultural beliefs is the need for harmony and balance, the interrelationships of the physical, psychological, emotional and spiritual parts of our being. We acknowledge that if one part of a person's being is out of balance, the other parts will be adversely affected. If a person grieves, it affects not only the psychological and emotional well-being, but also the physical and spiritual well-being. One aspect of being affects the whole. The collective consciousness of communities and families are affected in the same way. If the people's physical needs (shelter, food, economic well-being) are not being met, it will affect the psychological, emotional, and spiritual well-being of the community or the family. So we, in our collective consciousness, acknowledge that we must address all aspects of our collective harmony and balance (good jobs, decent housing, good parenting, respect of all living things, choices of where to attend school, community-based curriculum, elimination of alcoholism, drug abuse, and racism,) in order to solve all the social issues that remain in our communities and with our families. This need was eloquently expressed by Wayne Newell, a Passamaquaddy and one of our Lenape relatives (Cleary and Peacock, 1998, p. 101):

We have been trying to solve our community problems from the white value system. It's so simple that we never thought that maybe the solution is doing them according to the strong values within ourselves, and that if we do a good job in this generation, then the next generation will take over.

The Future of Indian Education and the Ojibwe Family
In the final chapter of Ignatia Broker's *Night Flying Woman,* Oona, the book's central character, wondered if today's children would ever want to know the stories and history of the People. As she sat in her chair, there came a knock on her door, and a little girl approached her. Oona asked her what she would like, and the little girl answered (Broker, 1983, p. 131), "I would like to hear the stories of our people." And with that, Oona knew the Ojibwe ways would live on forever.

So the future of Ojibwe people holds great promise. And like all visions, it will become real only if we live out its meaning and try to make it a reality. What might this future be? Hopefully, we will have more self-determined schools, free from the barrage of federal and state rules and regulations and free from the mandates of outside funding agencies, where Indian parents are empowered to create and develop their own learner-sensitive educational systems within the context of Ojibwe ways. Hopefully, decisions now made in Washington, Madison, Lansing, or St. Paul will be made in Bad River, Sault Ste. Marie, Red Lake, and other Ojibwe communities. Hopefully, we will deal with the loss of our Ojibwe language and move from the maintenance and enrichment programs we now have to full-blown language immersion programs. Moreover, we will hopefully confront the issues that prevent our communities and families from being in harmony and balance, and we will rely on solutions that lie within our communities, our culture, and ourselves.

GIKINOO'IMAWINDWAA
ABINOOJIINHYAG
(teaching the children)

Elders continue to pass down the Ojibwe ways to children.

Summary

THERE IS A NEED to return full circle to where this chapter began. I mentioned that, while reviewing central office files of the Bureau of Indian Affairs at the National Archives in Washington, I came upon a letter written by my great-grandmother, requesting that her son (my grandfather) not be sent to Pipestone Indian Boarding School because she was ill and needed his help at home that winter. A reply letter from some long dead Commissioner of Indian Affairs was attached, telling her my grandfather must report to the school as directed. Later, in reviewing other files, I was to find out my great-grandmother died that winter during a flu epidemic that swept the reservation. Finally, in reviewing other boarding school files, I came upon the "death files," folder after folder about children who had died in the federaln boarding schools that our great-grandparents, grandparents, and parents had been sent to in order to rid them of all vestiges of Ojibwe culture.

As Ojibwe people, one promise we can make to our great-grandparents, grandparents, and parents is to work to ensure that what happened to them will never happen again — not to our children nor to our children's children. We are deeply indebted to past generations for all they have suffered so that we could be here today, still strong in our ways. We can honor their memory by the way we live.

MASHKIIGOBAG
(Labrador tea)

Swamp tea

BIMAADIZIWIN
A Healthy Way of Life

Health and Medicine

I begin with an author's note. This chapter was difficult for me to write for several reasons. Traditional Ojibwe health practices, particularly those combined with prayer and ceremony, have been closeted in mystery for generations because they were banned for many years by the colonizers. Both governmental officials and agents of the church considered the ancient combination of herbal and spiritual care to be sorcery, so this subject is not one Ojibwe people openly discuss. Futhermore, some of us believe that to bring up unpleasant topics (or unpleasant spirits for that matter) is to will them.

An example:

On two occasions I was discussing the state of Ojibwe affairs, once with a brother and another time with a Passamaquaddy man I was interviewing. Both times a strange dog came to us and parked itself near where we were sitting. And both times the conversant and I looked at each other and said out loud,

"I think we are probably talking about something we shouldn't be talking about right now. Maybe we should change the subject."

And we did. To us, the dog was an emissary, a spirit in disguise, and it was there to tell us to change the subject.

A second major reason this was a difficult chapter to write is I am not a traditional health care practitioner. I know little about the subject except what I myself have experienced as a seeker of answers, a participant in an occasional ceremony, and an avid listener and reader. I am no expert at this and cannot pretend to be.

EACH DAY THAT PASSES reminds me that I am beginning to grow old. I know it because, when I look back at my early years (the 1950s), it seems so different from the world I live in today. One thing I remember is that my parents must have loved each other an awful lot (they had thirteen children). This was long before the advent of birth control, which wouldn't have mattered anyway because we were practicing Catholics (well, we went to church on Sundays, which is a far cry from what we do nowadays). The other thing I remember is that we, like most of the people on the reservation, were poor in a material sense. Some people remind me that we weren't simply poor; apparently, we were dirt poor. Today, when people of my generation tell each other stories about how poor everyone was back then (on my rez we say we are trying to "out poor" each other), my family always wins bragging rights. Our slop pail (a five-gallon pail) was used to pee and do other things (think of it as the precursor to indoor plumbing), and it would freeze over on cold winter evenings. Another sign of our poverty was our Christmas celebrations. Before Christmas our favorite toys would disappear, only to show up completely refurbished on Christmas day. Toy trucks would be repainted and have new sets of wheels. Ice skates would be freshly polished and sharpened and the runners would be repainted silver. My sisters' dolls would get new sets of clothes (homemade of course) and, if necessary, new arms and legs. I remember that sometimes these new appendages would be of various sizes and from various materials (some would be of hard or soft plastic and some of rubber). My mother would have lovingly scrubbed off the blue ink stitches and mustaches or beards that we boys had painted on the dolls. Few of these toys were store bought. Most were rummage sale specials or had been given to us by the church or some local charity. I resented the good intentions of charity back then. I still do.

So, back in those days, we didn't have the dime-store variety playthings. Sticks and boards would be carved into machine guns and used in war games. As usual, no one wanted to play the Indians (they always lost . . .). Bows and arrows were fashioned from hazelnut bushes, and red rubber slingshots took the place of BB guns.

I played with rocks; they were pretend cars. I would push them through the little dirt roads I had built, making squealing noises around all the corners, revving up the make-believe motors, and having pretend car crashes. My pretend cars would sometimes have pretend drivers who went on drunks. In my fantasies they drove down my pretend roads, going in and out of ditches and occasionally rolling over or hitting twigs (my pretend trees). And I know this sounds really crazy, but one time one of my rock cars found its way into one of my nostrils, which I was probably using as a pretend tunnel or as a hideout of some kind in one of my fantasies.

Well, anyway, it got stuck in there, and, no matter how hard I tried, it wouldn't come out. So off I went, crying to my mother and grandmother who tried in vain to extract it, using Vaseline as a lubricant to get that rock out of my nose. I remember sitting in a chair as they hovered over me, my grandmother with her tweezers and my mother holding my head. After a while, they decided to take me down to the Indian hospital. There, my "car" was finally removed, thanks to a skillful nurse with a pair of tweezers and long, white, skinny fingers with semi-sharp fingernails. My pretend car was promptly retrieved and put in a metal dish.

"Would you like to take it home with you?" she asked, peering down at me like a hawk, with her large, clean nostrils. I was crying and wiping off a slightly bloody nose and vigorously shaking my head.

"Uh, huh," I sobbed. I wanted it back.

My pretend cars never went into pretend tunnels again.

ONDAADIZIIKE KWE
(she was there at birth)

Elizabeth Thorne, an Ojibwe midwife from Sugar Island, Michigan

MISKWAADESI
(painted turtle)

The animals representative of the healing arts are the turtle and the otter.

A Chapter Road Map

IN A SENSE, MY GENERATION was one of transition from more traditional to contemporary times. Generations of Ojibwe children before me had toys fashioned from sticks and hides and rocks, and I am almost certain that, somewhere in the distant past, one of my ancestors got a rock stuck up his nostril as I did. They, however, didn't have an Indian hospital or a pair of tweezers or Vaseline, so who knows what was used for extraction purposes. They certainly didn't have access to the health care systems we have in many of our communities today.

This chapter is about health and wellness. It begins with a reminder to readers of the interrelationships of all things, of the need for harmony and balance as an integral part of the Ojibwe sense of wellness, of the recognition that we must attend not just to our physical selves, but also to the emotional and spiritual parts of our lives in order to be whole. It describes the traditional Ojibwe beliefs about and remedies for physical illnesses and the practice of the healing arts in modern times. Traditional Ojibwe remedies for emotional and spiritual wellness are discussed, as are their applications to contemporary times. It considers the state of Indian health from precontact with Europeans to the present, tracing the transitions all the way to the modern health care centers in contemporary Indian country. In doing so, it examines some key health issues facing the Ojibwe people of today — diabetes, obesity, heart disease, chemical abuse, and unresolved grief. Finally, it takes a hopeful look into the future, to a time when we have successfully dealt with the health and wellness issues facing the People and, thus, created communities where the strength and tenacity of our culture have returned us to who we once were — a strong and healthy people with a good sense of ourselves as individuals and as Ojibwe.

Reminders of the Interrelationships of the Physical, Emotional, and Spiritual Aspects of Wellness

The Ojibwe belief in the interrelationships of the physical, emotional, and spiritual selves is a fundamental aspect of our way of being, and the concept is just now being acknowledged in contemporary American society. Modern medicine is beginning to understand that the root of many physical ailments can be traced to emotional imbalances or spiritual vacuums. When people carry unresolved anger within themselves, they pass it on to others through their poor treatment of those with whom they interact. Moreover, if people do not relieve themselves of the anger, physical ailments will soon follow. Adults who carry the burden of unresolved grief pass it on to their children, where it surfaces in high rates of alcoholism, chemical abuse, and other forms of emotional illness. It is acknowledged that common complaints, such as headaches, are often caused by stress. People prone to clinical depression have high rates of cancer, heart disease, and other ailments. Those who do not attend to their spiritual needs are more prone to both physical and emotional afflictions. When elders who are confined to nursing homes and hospitals are visited on a regular basis by relatives, young people, or pets, they live longer and healthier lives and complain less about their physical ills. Stroking a pet lowers a person's blood pressure, a fact attested to by people who own cats and dogs. People relieve their stress and gain a better sense of well-being when they experience the affection and unconditional love of our animal partners, our elder brothers.

The relationship between physical and emotional healing was evidenced by a young man who appeared in my office one day on a personal journey in search of wisdom. When he left me that day, I knew his search for wisdom could not be fulfilled by talking to other people about wisdom and how to attain it, for the wisdom he sought was already there inside his heart. Perhaps by confronting his own fate, Scott Moore, a young cancer survivor, came to realize that both physical wellness and spiritual giving are the really important things we should be sharing (Moore and Brenning, 1997, p. 40):

Most of us have wills with which we pass on to others the little pieces of our material life that are left after we die. That's fine and good.

Meanwhile, days go by and we miss passing on to others the pieces of the inside of us that will mean more to others than anything we might write in our wills. There isn't a one of us who doesn't have some gift of living wisdom, some treasured part of ourselves, that we can share with someone else.

Medicine man's home and teepee, Grand Portage, 1925

Sharing pieces of your soul, that which makes you uniquely you, is what is truly important.

Elizabeth Pine of Sugar Island died in a flu epidemic during World War One. Many Ojibwe people died in epidemics that swept our communities.

TO OJIBWE PEOPLE, the earth is the mother of all life. She provides for us as the giver of life the plants used for healing purposes and the animals used for sustenance. Her sheer beauty is beneficial to our emotional and spiritual well-being, and many of us acknowledge our interrelationship with the earth on a daily basis. In all of this great circle that is life, there is an acknowledgment, a recognition, of the interconnectedness of all things and all people to the earth (Johnston, 1976, p. 26):

Mother Earth gives life; she takes it back. In pain, sickness and in sorrow a child turns to his mother for relief and comfort. A man or woman in suffering seeks repose upon the bosom of mother. They do not go to the father but turn to a woman for solace. All beings do this. Plants in dissolution bend before they collapse on the soil. Animal beings stricken by arrows or at last overcome by age lay down upon the ground. Men and women recline upon the earth in the final moments of life. It is then, as in birth, that children are closest to their mothers.

These interrelationships can best be illustrated when viewing our emotional and spiritual lives. I remember some time ago attending the funeral of an Ojibwe war veteran who was honored at a grave-side ceremony with a gun salute and the playing of "Taps" by the local chapter of the Veterans of Foreign War. As the priest stood praying over the casket and as his family grieved again, as they had too many times in the recent past, an eagle rose along the bluffs of the river that flows through Nagahchiwanong (Fond du Lac Reservation) and circled us. We all stood there and watched it for a long time.

"Do you see that eagle?" someone said. There was a hush and whispering among the gathered mourners. And then there was an acknowledgment and even slight smiles among many of the people. Until that time, the priest's chanting had little meaning for many of us. We only knew of a family's grieving, and we in turn grieved for the family. But the appearance of the eagle was a high honor to this man and to his family and a reminder to those of us who were there of our close relationship to the things of this earth. We walked away from that place with a renewed sense of hope and a sense of well-being and healing.

But there have been many, many other reminders of these interrelationships. A more recent reminder was the graduation ceremony of Indian people who had successfully completed chemical dependency treatment. In that sacred and healing place, I witnessed one of the most healing spiritual events I have ever attended, and I was overcome by the raw emotion, the sheer joy, of the event. There at Mashkawisen (Strength) Treatment Center in Sawyer, Minnesota, surrounded by Ojibwe people, during a pipe ceremony, and with a

Epidemic map shows some of the major epidemics that swept Ojibwe country.

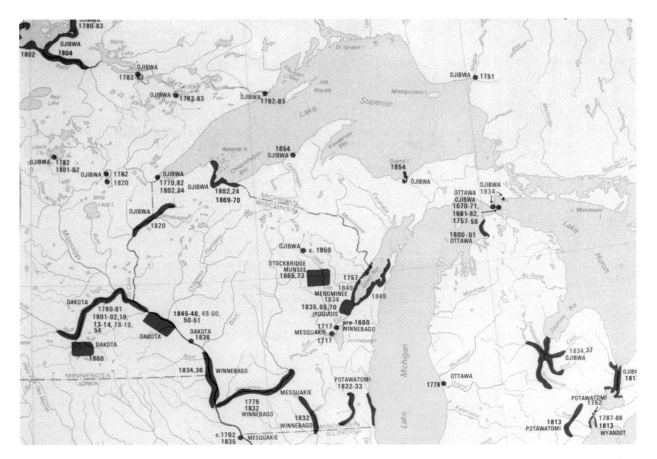

drum, I beheld for a moment, in the faces of those being honored, all the collective pain, which we have as a people, leave us. All the pain of past generations who were forced to sign treaties relinquishing our land, all the indignity of generations who became dependent on federal rations, all the sorrow of generations who were forced into boarding and mission schools, all the anger and degradation of generations who have been treated as second-class citizens in the country of their birth, all the despair of being harassed by the police and followed around in stores like common thieves, all the deep scars of physical and sexual abuse, all of the wrenching heartbreak left from brothers and sisters lost to car accidents and suicide and other unnatural passings — all of the collective grieving of our communities left us. For just that moment. For just that singular event. And I witnessed the power and healing of the Creator that day, and it shone in the faces of those being honored.

Traditional Notions of Health and Wellness

Another fundamental way of knowing among Ojibwe people is to perceive that there is little separation between everyday existence and things of the spirit. Spirits are all around us. In the time of our greatest need, we call upon the Creator and the spirits of our ancestors, our parents, our grandparents, and our aunties and uncles who have passed before us to give us solace and to be with us, to help us, and to guide us in making important decisions. When our children are ill, we attend to their physical needs and give them medicine. We also pray for their healing, and when they are in the greatest need, we consult with the Creator and our ancestors. There is little separation between our world and the spirit world. Understanding this concept is fundamental to understanding Ojibwe culture.

Medicine pole, Nett Lake, 1954

AAKOZIIWIGAMIG
(sick wigwam)

Indian hospital at White Earth, 1886. Hospitals were established on the reservations by the federal government in the late 1800s.

Our ancestors possessed great knowledge of the healing arts, which has been passed down through countless generations to the present time. In a time of great suffering, the Creator sent Waynabozho, the great uncle and teacher of the Ojibwe people, among them to give them knowledge of the healing arts. Waynabozho was part man and part spirit and had the characteristics of both. His strengths as a spirit brought much knowledge and great understanding about our relationships to the plants, animals, earth, and sky. Some of the knowledge is about the natural healing properties of plants. Other knowledge is about the importance of animals. The animals representative of the healing arts are the turtle and the otter. The turtle is used as the communicator between medicine people and the spirit world, and in ceremonies one can hear the voice of turtle as the intermediary, communicating between medicine people and the spirits. Medicine people speak to the spirit of turtle, who in turn speaks to other spirits, and then returns to humans with messages from the spirit world.

Traditional Health Care

Care of the young was of utmost importance in traditional communities, and one of the first things that was done was to give a name by a way'ay (namesake) to ensure the good health of a child. Sickly children might be given a second name by another person, in hopes they would become well. Hilger noted that (1992, p. 31): "Should a child take ill a second time and continue in its illness after medicinal remedies had been applied, it was given a third name by a third old person with all the ceremonials used when receiving its first name. A child might therefore have several names, receiving all but one for the restoration of health." The story of my son's naming provides an example of this important life event (Peacock, 1998, p. 291):

Hospital workers Liz Bear Smith and Donna May Smith are pictured standing in front of the Fond du Lac Indian Hospital.

When it was time for my children to receive their Indian names, my wife and I asked their Uncle Freddie Tonce, who was from Inger (in northern Minnesota on the Leech Lake Reservation). And we offered him tobacco and asked him if he would give names to them; and he said he would.

Now in the language of elders, a few weeks can mean anywhere from a week to a month or more, and it is part of our learning these things to know that. Never once have I heard one of the traditional elders say, "I'll be there next Sunday at 2:00 in the afternoon."

We saw him [Freddy Tonce] again when he was in Cass Lake, and he said he would be over to see us in a week. My wife prepared a feast of meat, wild rice, and fry bread; and we got a pouch of tobacco. He came over that day and gave the children their names. I remember him sitting there in the living room and asking the children to come over to him. He took them separately by both hands and talked to them in Ojibwe and in English. He talked about his dreams and gave them their names. We set out a separate plate of food with some tobacco, which was later brought out into the woods.

Later I said of my boy's name, "What does it mean?" and he said, "You are walking in the woods, and, out of the corner of your eye, you see a wolf. And you look toward where it should be and it is not there."

MAAZHIPOGWAD MASHKIKI
(bad tasting medicine)

A child receiving medicine at the WPA Indian Nursery School on Nett Lake Reservation, 1938. Health care was often administered to children through the schools.

Good thing that name is in Ojibwe.

Decisions about what would be used to treat sicknesses of various sorts were dependent upon what was felt to be the source of affliction. If it was determined that the source was from natural causes, then natural cures (herbs, medicines, and preventive measures) were found, just as in modern health care. Some of these age-old herbal medicines are still in common use throughout Ojibwe country. We-kay (bitterroot) is used for sore throats. Many drummers at

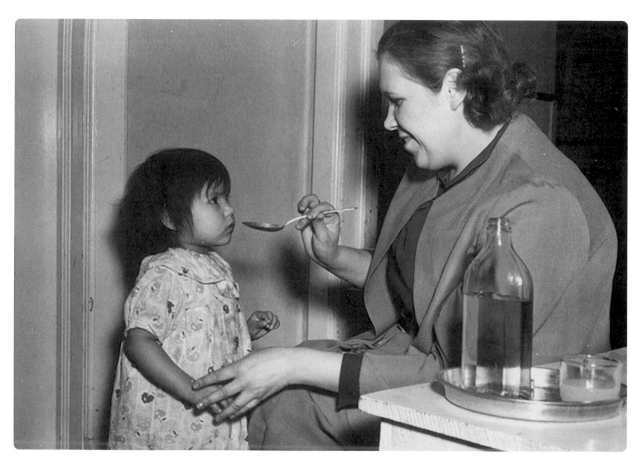

Indian Health Service diphtheria
immunization clinic, ca. 1930

contemporary pow-wows can be found chewing we-kay to keep
from getting a sore throat or losing their voice. Squirrel tail is used
to coagulate the blood; it is chewed and put as a poultice on a
wound to stop bleeding. Swamp tea is brewed for colds. Other
similar remedies are described by Hilger (1992, p. 92):

*Skin eruptions are sponged with a decoction made by boiling strawberry roots and
alum. Dried resin, ground to powder, is dusted on skin sores. Chewing the root
of sweet flag (wi'bank'), gathered late in fall after growth has stopped, cures sore
throats. Decoctions of the roots of wild celery is thought to cure tuberculosis; the
leaves of "zens" stop sweating that occurs with colds; flowers of the boneset, if
picked "just before the frost sets in," subdues a fever; sturgeon potatoes (nama'pin),
gathered in the fall when they are filled with strength, cure heart trouble; mixing a
root found in swamps (mackwo'kawac) and catnip (namewac') revives fainting
persons or quickens weak heart beats.*

If the affliction was felt to be from spiritual sources, however, the
afflicted or family members would consult a medicine person. Sometimes
a person was taken to a bone doctor (Hilger, 1992, p. 89):

*Suppose there is something wrong in the chest or some part of the body. You call
in a medicine man. He has the bones of a bird, for example, a goose, the largest
ones of which are probably 2 inches long. He will have two or three of these bones,
cleaned and smoothed. When he is ready to perform on the patient, he puts the
bones into a dish of clean water. One by one, he puts them into his mouth and
swallows them. He then puts his mouth on the chest, or on the bare skin of the
sick part, and one by one he will cough up the bones. He sucks the sick part
through the bones, and sometimes worms of whatever the sickness appear. [Hilger,
1936 c, pp. 45-46.]*

Doctoring, as it is often called today, is becoming more and
more rare in Ojibwe country. The scarcity is a result of the decline
in Ojibwe language fluency (all the ceremonies are done in the
indigenous language) and the cultural vacuum left during the period

Indian hospital at Pipestone School, 1928

when these skills were not being handed down through the generations. Medicine people sometimes still come all the way from Canada to visit Ojibwe communities. They travel throughout Ojibwe country via an informal network of traditional people, who let each other know when the medicine person will be in town and how to make arrangements for seeing this person. Some contemporary health care providers, including the clinic on my own reservation, still make arrangements for people who want to consult with traditional medicine people. They are among the most highly respected members of our communities because they are the purveyors and keepers of ancient sacred knowledge.

At rare times when the root cause of an emotional, spiritual, or physical affliction or a combination of ailments cannot be readily assessed, other special ceremonies (sometimes called "tipi shaking" or jeezakkid) might be held (Hilger, 1992, pp. 77–78):

Indian health camp, 1940. Summer camps were held to teach students health practices. This one also provided some cultural activities.

A medicine man may be called on, day or night, to discover the cause and the cure of some internal disease. The sick man is placed on a mat outside the small wigwam in which the medicine man is exercising his powers. All during the ceremony someone on the outside beats the drum. It is absolutely necessary that the wigwam sway back and forth, for, without it, the procedure is ineffective. As soon as the tipi shakes — which indicates the spirits are in the wigwam — the medicine man asks the persons on the outside who are interested in the sick man what they wish to know. The spirits on the inside answer. One can hear them talking but only the man in the wigwam usually understands the language, for only occasionally do the spirits speak Chippewa [Ojibwe]. The voices sound like those of a large crowd. It's these spirits that make the wigwam sway.

These ceremonies are not held just for ailments of various sorts; it is sometimes necessary to consult the spirits for advice, for direction, or for permission to do certain things. As these ceremonies continue, often late into the evening, each individual seeking spiritual guidance comes before the wigwam. Some have physical ailments. Others are there for consultation on the physical ailments of relatives. Some are there for emotional pain, be it alcoholism or family or marital strife. Others are there with important life questions and are in need of spiritual direction. The people are there for their individual reasons. And the spirits provide answers.

Rez Pharmacies

The indigenous people of this continent knew much about the practice of healing with traditional herbs and medicines, and their contributions to modern medicine are just now being recognized. While under standing of the healing properties of plants was brought to the Ojibwe by Waynabozho, knowledge was also attained by observing animals, the elder brothers. Johnston (1976, p. 41) described such a drama. In the story, a little girl and her grandmother were out picking blueberries in the woods.

As they made their way along the lush patches of berries, the grandmother abruptly halted, pointed to the ground, and whispered to the granddaughter, "Watch, you will never see this again."

The little girl looked to the ground where the grandmother pointed. There in the grasses was a snake pursuing a small green frog. Little girl and aged woman watched the drama on the ground. The snake was gaining but before he could seize the frog in his jaws, the frightened quarry leaped into a grove of poison ivy.

There the frog remained because it knew the snake would not follow. It did not move until long after the snake had left in disappointment. Johnston told the rest of the story:

Once out of the poison ivy the little frog fairly flew over the ground bounding without pause until he came to another grove of plants. Within that grove of jewel weed, the little frog twisted and turned and writhed washing every part of himself.

From the conduct of the little frog, the Anishinabeg learned the cure for poison ivy. Such knowledge has today found its way into our pharmacies, where medicines long used by indigenous people are

ISHKIINZHIGOJIIBIK
(eye root)

Jack in the pulpit was used for diseases of the eye.

ININIWINDIBIGEGAN
(trillium)

Trillium was used for diseases of the ear and joints.

Giiziso-mashkiki
(Golden rod)

The Ojibwe people used plants to treat a variety of illnesses and conditions. Golden rod was used for lung and digestive problems, burns, fever, ulcers, and boils.

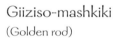

prescribed by health care providers all over the world. The short list of contributions (Weatherford, 1988, pp. 175–196):

— Quinine, found in Peruvian bark and used to treat the symptoms of malaria. Commonly drunk in tonic water, used as a mixer, and sold throughout the world.

— Sassafras and sarsaparilla teas, used for various ailments, and now mixed with sugar and carbonated water and called "root beer."

— Ipecac, made from the root and relative of the same tree from which quinine is extracted, is used worldwide to induce vomiting and to expel poisons and other unwanted substances. Ipecac is most widely known, however, for curing amoebic dysentery, a long-time killer of the young.

— Massive doses of vitamin C from hemlock or pine or cranberries to cure scurvy.

— The most commonly used laxative, made from the bark of a shrub, Rhamnus purshiana, and called "sacred bark" by the Spaniards because it relieved constipation so well.

— Curare, once used to poison the tips of arrows in South America, used today in euthanasia and as a muscle relaxant.

— Aspirin, the most commonly used pain and fever reducer in the world, is used for everything from simple headaches to reducing the risk of heart attacks because of its effectiveness as a blood thinner and anticoagulant.

— Cocaine (from the leaves of the coca bush), first used as an anesthetic and stimulant, now as a drug of choice among the drug cult, and at one time, an ingredient in the most common soft drink in the world, Coca-Cola.

Other herbal remedies are described by Weatherford (1988, p. 185):

Indians in the northeastern United States treated intestinal worms with the vermifuge pinkroot, Spigelia marilandica, a plant with red and yellow flowers. Trees of the genus Cornus of North America, known as dogwoods, were used by the Indians as febrifuge, or fever reducer. They had a number of emetics in addition to ipecac; these included bloodroot — Sanguinaria canadensis, also called puccoon — and lobelia. The Indians made an astringent called alumroot from the wild geranium, Heuchera americana, and a stimulant from boneset, Eupatorium perfoliatum.

Other remedies included treatments to help induce the menstrual cycle (Caulophyllum thalictroides, from the roots of oak trees), witch hazel (tired or strained muscles), and petroleum jelly (the world's most commonly used skin ointment). Perhaps the least known but most beneficial of all health preventive measures was the practice of frequent bathing, which was common to nearly all indigenous groups on both the northern and southern continents of the Americas. Bathing was abhorred in Europe, where it was thought that bathing too frequently led to diseases and where perfumes were used to mask human body odor (Weatherford, 1988, pp. 186–187, 189–190).

Napoleon Ross (Fond du Lac) purified group members with cedar and sage at Mash-ka-wisen Treatment Center, Fond du Lac, 1991.

The State of Health and Wellness in Ojibwe Country

Ojibwe health and wellness concerns can be divided into two categories — dietary and nutrition, and emotional and spiritual. All are intricately interrelated, and we will need a multi-front response to eradicate the multiple health and wellness issues that affect our communities.

Nutrition and exercise, or the lack thereof

Indian tacos (fry bread smothered with a variety of favorite taco fillings) and I have been intimate friends for most of my life, so I know health and wellness issues primarily from the perspective of a consumer. My family history would make for a wonderful poster on how not to live, what not to eat, what not to drink, how to not exercise, and what smoking or drinking or taking dangerous risks can do to oneself. The list of issues might make for a couple of posters. But I am not alone here. The same issues that have plagued my family are common in many Ojibwe families. These concerns keep our health and social service centers busy and legions of human service and health care professionals employed. No wonder health care is a growth industry.

Traditional Ojibwe people had diets high in fiber (corn, squash, pumpkins, beans, acorns, strawberries, blueberries, June berries, choke cherries, cranberries, Indian turnips, milkweed) and low in fat (fish of all sorts, wild rice, deer, moose, bear, buffalo, rabbits, partridge, porcupines, skunks, ducks, geese, pigeons, beaver, muskrat, and other critters). Certain meat was avoided (wolf), and turtles were eaten only by men. Turtle eggs were prized. Sugar (maple syrup) was unprocessed and easily digestible. Beverages made with raspberry or wintergreen leaves or "swamp" tea washed things down. Moreover, the people did hard physical labor in order to survive. Without amenities such as cars and central heat and electricity, this is still an unforgiving land. So in traditional times, there were no "fry breaders" (what we Ojibwe call obese people). The People were fit.

Since the first delivery of government rations, things have changed. Our diets now contain foods high in saturated fat (primarily from eating beef), toxins of various sorts (chemicals, dyes, and other poisons added to processed foods), processed sugars, dairy products (despite the fact that lactose intolerance is common in Indian country), and foods high in carbohydrates (too many potatoes, too much white rice). So many of us lumber around the rez, and we die young from the effects of obesity, including heart disease and adult onset diabetes. And far too many of us finish our meals with a cigarette, increasing the probability of a heart attack or lung cancer.

Issues of emotional and spiritual health

A more complicated health issue is the cumulative negative effect of being American Indian in a non-Indian world. American Indians are faced with oppression from the non-Indian world (institutional racism, overt and covert racism, malfunctioning institutions that purport to serve Indian people, communities in trouble), which leads to an internalization of oppression (Cleary and Peacock, 1998, p. 63):

Continued oppression eventually turns the oppressed against each other, and in these instances a twisted form of self-hate develops in the oppressed until eventually they internalize their oppression and become the suboppressor. History is replete with blatant examples of this. Some of the best scouts in the U.S. cavalry used against American Indian nations were fellow American Indians. The most feared guards in the Nazi death camps were fellow Jews. The suboppressor is another form of oppression.

Jimmy Jackson, a highly respected Ojibwe spiritual leader, 1977

THE MASHKA-WISEN
(Be Strong)

Sobriety Pow-wow is celebrated every year on the Fond du Lac Reservation.

Examples of this self-hate are evident in some of our Ojibwe communities today. We are just now emerging from a period when some Ojibwe people were ashamed of their indigenous heritage. Instead of being proud of their heritage, they would say they were Italian or French-Canadian, or they said nothing at all. But we see other examples in our communities today: institutional abuse from bureaucratic structures (i.e. personnel policies that favor the hiring of non-Indians over Indians for jobs in Indian programs, income eligibility requirements set by outside funding agencies that screen out people who really need assistance); white privilege (an example would be when we heed the expertise of non-Indians over our own experts or when we show non-Indians more personal respect than we do our own people); destructive personality politics and the abuse of power at some governmental and institutional levels.

The effects of internalized oppression take their toll in Ojibwe country (Cleary and Peacock, 1998, p. 63):

There is a need, however, to expand this view of the suboppressor to encompass the more subtle oppression of one's self, because the suboppressor will also try to destroy his or her own self through acts of self-destruction: alcoholism, drug abuse, suicide, and the other vestiges of internalized oppression. The problems with alcoholism and the abnormally high rates of suicide in some American Indian communities are examples of internalized oppression.

Finally, the self-destructive nature of internalized oppression affects our need for harmony and balance (Cleary and Peacock, 1998, p. 64):

The self-destructive nature of this suboppressive behavior has an impact on our need for harmony and balance, which is an integral characteristic of the philosophy of many American Indian tribes. The lack of balance in an individual can grow to adversely affect families, communities and whole tribes. For example, if an individual carries the burden of anger in them, that anger will affect the other parts of their being; their spiritual well-being and their physical health may eventually be impaired. Anger may affect their relationships with others, including family members, and in doing so will adversely affect the harmony and balance of the family. It may eventually affect their relationships with others at school or work, or may cause groups in a tribe to be in friction with one another, and upset the harmony of the community's institutions. Unresolved anger is one of the most self-destructive elements of the suboppressor.

A final result of generations of oppression and internalized oppression is the unresolved grief in so many individuals, families, and communities. Ojibwe country is filled with a kind of irony, a fact so eloquently put by Linda LeGarde Grover (Grand Portage Band of Lake Superior Chippewa), who noted that among Indian people where there is great happiness, there is also great sorrow. Where there is great sorrow, there is great happiness. And we have adapted that way in order to live our lives. Too many of us have buried our brothers and sisters, aunties and uncles and cousins, and our own children because of suicide and car accidents and violent crime and alcohol poisoning and from the cumulative anger and grief itself. Yet through all of this we remain a people with a good sense of humor. Where there are Indians there is unrestrained laughter. There is nothing like Indian humor. We are always laughing, especially at ourselves. Physical

Kathy Smart, R. N., of Bad River pictured at the Ashland, Wisconsin, hospital

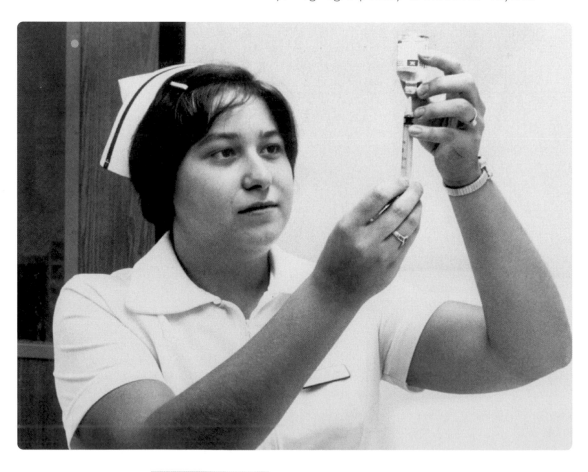

Dr. Arne Vainio, a physician and a White Earth band member, educates children about health-care issues.

humor rules: If someone bumps his head, we laugh. If someone bugats (passes gas), we laugh even louder. If we trick someone with a practical joke, it's roll-on-the-floor laughing time. We have survived this horrible period of history with our sense of humor.

Contemporary Responses to Health and Wellness Issues

Americans, in general, are blessed by having the best health care in the world; however, until a few years ago, the indigenous people of this country suffered from a lack of adequate health care. This has changed. Many Ojibwe communities now have their own ambulatory clinics, and specialized services are available to many people in both reservation and urban Indian communities. Modern comprehensive health care facilities dot Ojibwe country. A few reservations, like Red Lake (northern Minnesota), boast new hospitals. Primary treatment centers, like Mashkawisen in Sawyer, Minnesota, have helped many Ojibwe people again walk the good path. Urban clinics in all the major cities where Ojibwe people live (Milwaukee, Minneapolis, Duluth) provide for the health needs of the majority of Ojibwe people who do not reside on or near reservation areas.

In some reservation areas, the health needs of our animal brothers are also provided for. While staying at a brother's home several years ago, I saw an Indian Public Health Service van pull into the housing project and begin vaccinating cats and dogs for rabies and distemper. Seeing an old rez dog parked in my brother's yard, I coaxed and carried and pulled and pushed the animal over to the van, where it was given its shots. Later, I told my brother of my good deed, and he responded, "I don't have a dog."

I wonder whose dog I got vaccinated that day.

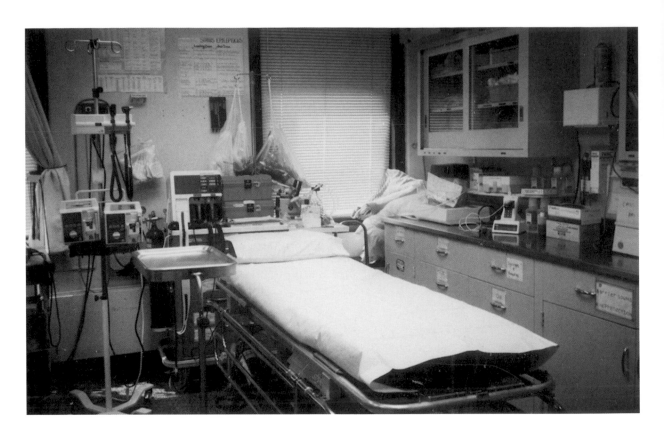

Modern health service facilities such as this one at Cass Lake Indian Hospital now serve many Ojibwe communities.

Summary

I BEGAN THIS CHAPTER with the story of when I got a rock stuck in my nose (some would say I still have rocks in my head) and had to go to the old Indian hospital that once stood in a field near the old government farm on the Fond du Lac Reservation. There, a nurse with long, skinny white fingers removed it from my nose. I remember taking the rock home with me that day, and when I got out of our old rez car with the removable back seat (it was used as a wood hauler, too), I threw it as far as I could. I can still see it flying through the air, spinning slowly, arching over bushes and into a deep cleave in the woods. And the funny thing is, it is still out there somewhere, within feet of where I live today. Waiting for me.

As a people we have survived the darkest chapter of our existence, that period just following colonization when we were subjected to repressive governmental and church efforts to rid us of all vestiges of our Ojibwe ways. The resultant loss of culture, including traditional health and wellness practices, is conveyed by Broker when she describes the generations of Ojibwe sent to boarding school (1983, p. 125):

They danced the powwow and did the beadwork because these were expected of them by the tourists from the east. They did the planting and harvesting, the blueberry picking and the ricing, for these were necessary. But they never stood with eyes cast down before the Old Ones to ask about the old ways and the old people. They never offered the first of the harvest. They did not respect the Mi-de-wi-wi-n people. Instead they feared them. They never knew the forest trails and the animal people. They never gathered herbs and medicine or listened to the si-si-gwa-d [the murmuring that trees make].

But just like Broker's *Night Flying Woman*, which describes how a young girl stood before Oona (the lead character) and asked for the wisdom of the old stories, the Ojibwe, too, are becoming whole as a people again. The greatest of triumphs is our survival from these dark times and the fact that we again stand proud and free before the Creator as both individuals and communities who are beginning to live healthy, purposeful lives. The People once again stand before the Old Ones with eyes cast down, and they are again beginning to recognize that all things of this universe, from the tiniest bits of matter to the farthest star, are all interconnected, all part of a great and wondrous story in the weaving (Big Eagle, 1983, p. 22):

My Grandfather Was A Quantum Physicist

I can see him now
smiling
in full dance costume
with other men
in front of the roundhouse
on a sunny afternoon.

Scientists have finally discovered
that the intimate details
of our lives
are influenced by things
beyond the stars
and beyond time.

My grandfather knew this.

While we still have a long recovery process, there are many more Ojibwe who are facing in the right direction and walking the good path than ones who are not. Happy faces can be seen at pow-wows. Joy is in the eyes of our babies in Head Start centers and at tribal health fairs and family camps. The Creator's hand is firmly on our shoulders during the graduation ceremonies at our treatment centers. More people are listening to their elders and medicine people. All of this is part of a story of our own weaving, a story in which we are both the storytellers and the characters of the story, a story where the ending is a good one because we are writers of the conclusion. All of this is good.

White birch trees

WADENA

Chief of Mille Lacs (on the left) with elders smoking
in council, about 1900

GWAYAKOCHIGEWIN
Doing Things the Right Way

Traditionally, Ojibway leaders were accepted by the tribe for some immediate purpose and were followed only so long as they fulfilled it. No permanent commitment was made to a leader or to a highly centralized authority system. Because traders and government officials preferred to deal with as few people as possible, however, a "leader" was designated for transactions with outsiders. Emergence of permanent leadership, some believe, was the creation of white economic control and influence, not necessarily the result of developments within the tribal culture itself.

— *Elizabeth Ebbott*, Indians of Minnesota

Governance and Leaders

My brother Sonny has been the tribal chairman of my home reservation for many years. Before becoming chairman, he was the reservation's chief executive (executive director), and before that he was a district representative on the tribal council. Before that he was a typical reservation Indian, just like me. I have sat at his kitchen table on most tribal election nights (and it's odd, but I have been the only one there with him) as he awaited word from the council chambers where "his people" were following the counting of ballots to see if he was going to remain in office or if he was going to become a typical reservation Indian again. I have witnessed his leadership as he has led the reservation from a ten-million dollar debt, incurred because of bad financial decisions, to the casino revenue we seem to be drowning in today. While realizing that casino gambling may well be a passing phenomenon, he sometimes wonders how it all came to be, saying of himself, "I am like a little kid in a candy store. Not only do I get to buy all the candy I want, but I *own* the machines that make the candy." We grew up in tar paper shacks, so it is a long way from getting shagged out of penny candy stores to owning both the store and the candy factory.

Several years ago, a significant faction of his detractors staged a protest of the reservation's spending of casino revenue for a new tribal center, which came to be called "Camp Truth." Set up in the pow-wow grounds, the camp became a daily gathering place for anti-tribal government protestors, new-age pan-Indian traditionalists, old-age Indian hippies, self-appointed Indian spokespersons, and oppressed former tribal politicians ('outies') who wanted to re-enter tribal politics so they could become 'innies' and oppress their oppressors. Daily activities of the odd collection of malcontents were captured on video by several van loads of the non-Indian television media. Needless to say, it was a very tense several months, as family members were

SINGABA W'OSSIN
(Image Stone)

Early leader of the Ojibwe at St. Mary's, Michigan

BESHEKE

Chief Buffalo, leader of La Pointe in the mid-1800s. Descendants of Buffalo still provide leadership in Ojibwe country as tribal leaders and attorneys.

threatened or felt threatened and as reservation people who really didn't like each other chose sides and came to really dislike each other.

A minority of protestors became violent and did some random shootings, and several homes and vehicles were burned during the protest; so, we were forced into a survival mode. We kept our rifles loaded and by our bedsides at nights. I taught my kids not to sit near the windows, so as not to invite a drive-by shooter. I hated what the protest was doing to me, and I hated all the stress I felt because the protestors were threatening my family. To this day, when I see the former protest leaders in the local stores, I feel an intense surge of anger. I need to forgive them, but my own anger betrays me. And I think of the time on the reservation when my generation was growing up: when we were all poor and the only thing we had to fight about was being poor and having nothing; when there was no class system and hence no large disparities between the have's and have nots; when there were no prestigious or high-paying jobs to compete over; and when there were no programs or casinos with large budgets to lord over. I am not saying that things were better then, because they were not. It's just that we've come such a long way and have gone nowhere, all at the same time.

Sonny has been wondering if the last election was his final run for chairman. He sometimes says he wants to retire from politics and become a 'greeter' (like a Wal-Mart greeter?) at the reservation's golf course/ hotel complex. I hope that by then we have matured on our reservation where his replacement on the council hires him to be a greeter, or hires him for any position for that matter. I am hoping for the day when we move away from the intense politicization of the reservation, a day when jobs and services are no longer the rewards for the victors and the defeated are no longer vanquished.

BUG-O-NAY-GE-SHIG
(Hole-In-The-Day)

Leader of Gull Lake band

Flat Mouth was a Pillager leader in battles against the Dakota.

A Chapter Road Map

AJIJAAK
(sand hill crane)

Of all the echo-makers, the crane was preeminent and for this reason was selected to symbolize leadership and direction.

THE CHAPTER BEGINS with a description of leadership in traditional Ojibwe society, that long span of time before contact with non-Indians when Ojibwe society was dominated by dodaim (clans) and ways of leading and following were egalitarian. It offers a brief discussion of the impact of Indigenous governance on American democracy. It explains how contact with Europeans led to the necessary emergence of new types of leaders as politicians (spokespersons who were the primary agents of interaction between the Ojibwe and non-Indian world). Examples of some traditional Ojibwe leaders from the period of colonization are given — Buffalo, Bugonaygeshig, and others. It provides a rare glimpse of the leadership provided by warriors and traditional Ojibwe medicine people. Issues of self-determination and governance, sovereignty, federal court cases, and laws and policies are introduced from the perspective of their influence on the development of modern tribal government. In doing so the chapter covers the period of Indian reorganization and the development of modern Indian leadership during the period of self-determination. It follows the evolution of leadership to contemporary times and give examples of several contemporary Ojibwe leaders whose presence has had a lasting impact in Indian country. Finally, it speculates on Indian leaders and governance in the future and presents a vision of a postmodern governance that may combine both traditional and contemporary governing characteristics.

Leadership in Traditional Ojibwe Communities

In traditional Ojibwe society, persons born in the bird clans (crane, goose, loon, hawk, sparrow hawk, white-headed eagle, black-headed eagle, brant, seagull) were given training for their future duties (Johnston, 1976, p. 63):

In preparation, they studied history, tradition, grammar, and speaking. Part of the training fostered eloquence, wisdom, and generosity. It was hoped that such training would inculcate in the tentative candidate a special deference to the principle that in government the well being of the people superseded all other considerations.

Johnston's description of the clan system in traditional Ojibwe society offers a wonderful metaphor of the crane as the symbol of leadership (Johnston, 1976, p. 61):

Of all the echo-makers the crane was most eminent and for this reason was selected to symbolize leadership and direction. The call that it uttered was as infrequent as it was unique. So unusual was the tone and pitch of the voice that all the other creatures suspended their own utterances to harken to the crane. When the crane calls, all listen.

As the crane calls infrequently and commands attention, so ought a leader to exercise his prerogative rarely and bear the same attention in the discharge of his duties. He speaks infrequently lest he be considered shallow. A leader having no other source of authority except for the force of character and persuasion did not jeopardize his tenuous ability. Moreover, a leader was not merely a commander, but was first in action; and as a speaker, he did not utter his own sentiments, but those of his people. As such, the leader was obligated to shield the feelings of his people and not to depreciate them by too frequent speech. He was as leader an example and the first of speakers only.

Johnston goes on to describe traditional Ojibwe leadership as something exercised temporarily. He uses bird migration as a metaphor for this, indicating that in the fall the birds need a leader to migrate south, and in the spring they seek leadership to return to the north. When the need is ended, according to Johnston, so is the

MONGAZID

Loonsfoot, leader at Fond du Lac

SHOPPENAGON

Michigan Ojibwe chief, with his wife and daughter

leadership. Other principles described include (Johnston, 1976, p. 61-63):
— Followers followed freely and could withdraw at any time. No coercion was used to keep people part of the flock.
— There were many leaders in the small bands that made up the great Ojibwe nation. There was no single leader.
— There was no contest for who would be leader. Leadership was considered a burden, not something to be sought.

Leadership did not, however, come just from the ranks of the bird clans. If other young people showed promise, they would be given leadership training. And upon being made a leader, the person so chosen was expected to work with a council of people, men and women of the community and elders. Hereditary chiefs, war chiefs, and clan leaders were part of these councils. Their duties included acting as a panel to judge wrong-doing, settle individual and family disputes, allocate hunting and fishing territories, decide where and when to move the community with the seasons, and make decisions on issues of peace or war.

Traditional Ojibwe leaders emerged in times when their areas of expertise would be most useful to the tribe (Peacock, 1989). Accordingly, persons who were skilled hunters became leaders during hunting time. Great warriors became leaders when it was time to go to war with other tribes. Persons who could speak English or French and could interact with non-Indians emerged during the period of colonization. Once the task that needed to be dealt with was completed, the person returned to the group as an equal. Leadership was temporary and shared. The use of temporary leaders based upon expertise became an issue when British (and later American) colonizers selected Indians as "chiefs" for treaty signing and other purposes when there was an unwillingness on the part of traditional Indian leaders to cooperate with federal officials.

The egalitarian ethos was also recognized in our Lenape relatives, according to Williamson (1832):

Such were the exalted ideas of liberty, that they had no word by which to express our meaning of subject; and the character of master formed, in their view, some attribute of a demon. . . . Here was a civil freedom and an equality of rights, though not of rank.

WA-BON-O-QUOT

Chief White Cloud, leader at White Earth, in 1895

Influences of American Indians on American Democracy

While the Ojibwe form of governance was not as well defined as in other tribes, it shared some governance characteristics with other tribal nations. For example, much of the decision-making responsibility was made at the band/community level, with little in the way of a national government. Caucusing, negotiating, and compromising were accepted standard practice in tribal politics. Leaders were not considered part of a power elite but stood as equals with other members of the community.

The democratic form of American government was modeled after the Iroquois Confederacy, which united the Mohawk, Onondaga, Seneca, Oneida, and Cayuga nations (Weatherford, 1988, p. 136):

Speaking to the Albany Congress in 1754, [Benjamin] Franklin called on the delegates of the various English colonies to unite and emulate the Iroquois League, a call that was not heeded until the Constitution was written three decades later.

The Iroquois Confederation was formed into what is today known as the "federal" system of government, with each individual nation having its own government but also united with a larger council. This pattern was used for the individual states and the formation of the federal government. Other Iroquois beliefs the colonists followed include: separating military and civil leadership; impeachment to remove someone from office; having a process for incorporating new member nation/states; allowing individuals to speak at political gatherings without interruption (which is contrary to the raucous British political discussions); the use of compromise and negotiation to settle political disputes; the supreme authority of the group rather than the individual; free elections; and the caucus.

MAJI GA BOW

Chief of the Bear Island Pillagers in the late 1800s

Ojibwe Chiefs at Lake of the Woods in 1922

The Warrior Leader

In reading Warren's *History of the Ojibway People* one might be led to believe the Ojibwe were a people in a constant state of war; however, Warren's historical perspective focused heavily on conflicts with the Dakota, Fox, and Iroquois. In truth, our ancestors were a peaceful people who waged war only in rare circumstances. Never was war made to acquire the land or resources of others, nor to subjugate others; war was a means to avenge a death or an injury. Because of the intense personal nature of war missions, warriors and their leaders were feared (Johnston, 1982, p. 59):

Battles between tribes were thus essentially the result of a need for revenge. They seldom involved a large number of warriors and, because they were similar to hit and run raids, they rarely lasted beyond half a day. Conflict was personal rather than tribal, and was undertaken with a fierce sense of duty. It was because of this devotion to the avenging of wrongs, with no regard for consequences, that warriors were feared.

Warrior leaders often sent messengers or made journeys themselves to other villages to gather warriors in preparation for battle. There was no strong sense of national unity, or clan unity for that matter, in the making of war. Conflicts were limited, infrequent, personal, and intense.

Historic Ojibwe Leaders

Many of the details of the ancient past lie beyond our memory or the memory provided in our stories. We will never know the stories of the people who led our ancestors on the various migrations, nor the stories of those who led the People in war against our traditional enemies of the East, nor the stories of those who saved our communities from disease and starvation. As descendants of those great people, we carry their genetic material and fragments of ancestral

Peter Graves, long-time Red Lake leader, 1950.

"We believe the greatest evil the government ever inflicted on the Indians was to allot lands in severalty to them. There are some of us who believe that if we take land in severalty on the Red Lake reservation, our doom is sealed."

memory (which are sometimes revealed in dreams or intuition), but their names and the stories of their lives are forever lost. Their lives may have been like mountains, but we know nothing of them, or only grains of sand. And that, it seems, is one of the tasks of contemporary Ojibwe writers and historians: To take these bits of historical and cultural knowledge and put them back into their proper places, grain by grain, until they form the true story of the Ojibwe people.

We do know the stories of leaders from the more recent past (within the last several hundred years), primarily those who led us during the period of colonization and treaty making. Many of them were leaders in a true sense. Others were only written about, and their life stories have been interpreted to make them heroes or leaders. That is the nature of our recent history, which has been interpreted and captured in words by the colonizers and by those who have been colonized; we will never know the full story from the perspective of Ojibwe people themselves. Moreover, much of what has been written focused on European colonization and war. The stories of the lives and deeds of these leaders appear in trader and Jesuit journals and by the historians Schoolcraft and Warren. Some of the leaders include (Warren, 1984):

— Besheke (Buffalo): principal chief of LaPointe (Red Cliff and Bad River areas) in the mid-1800s. Descendants of Buffalo still provide leadership in Ojibwe country as tribal leaders and attorneys.

— Waubojeeg (White Fisher): leader of LaPointe who refused to be drawn into the war between the European powers in 1754-63. He led the People in war against the Dakota and Fox. Both Schoolcraft and Warren wrote about his life.

— Bugonaygeshig (Hole in the Day): the first Hole in the Day was involved in treaty making in the mid-1800s. The second Bugonaygeshig led the last armed struggle of Indian people against American forces in 1898 on the Leech Lake Reservation.

— Flat Mouth: a Pillager chief who led in battle against the Dakota.

— Wasson: a war leader of the Saginaw Bay area, who helped defeat the British in one of the first French-Indian battles.

— Kishkimun (Sharpened Stone): led the Crane clan to Lac du Flambeau.

— Babesigaundibay (Curly Head): a Sandy Lake war chief in the early 1800s.

Contemporary Leadership and Governance

Contemporary leadership and governance in Ojibwe country is an intricate blend of Ojibwe tradition and representative democracy modeled after the American government, which in turn was patterned after the Iroquois Confederacy. This complex topic deserves more extensive treatment than this cursory examination can offer. Thousands of laws, hundreds of treaties, and innumerable administrative rulings and actions have come to define the federal-Indian relationship (Deloria and Lytle, 1984). Whole books have been devoted to issues inherent in the tribal-federal situation and questions of sovereignty. Among them are Pevar's *The Rights of Indians and Tribes*, Cohen's *Federal Indian Law*, and Deloria and Lytle's *The Nations Within*. Given the nature of the ongoing struggle of tribes to maintain their limited sovereignty in the face of state and federal challenges, the final chapter on this topic has yet to be written.

Sovereign Nations

At the heart of Ojibwe governance is an understanding of the federal-Indian relationship and the notion of tribal sovereignty (tribes as sovereign domestic nations within a larger United States). When the English, and later the Americans, negotiated treaties with Indian nations, they negotiated on a government-to-government basis. The recognition that tribes have limited rights of sovereignty as nations is what separates tribal members from all other citizens of this country. It is a policy defined by the Constitution and upheld in court decisions. Indians are dual citizens of tribal nations and of the United States. This right was affirmed in the historic U.S. Supreme Court case, Worcester vs. Georgia of 1832 (Deloria and Lytle, 1984, p. 16):

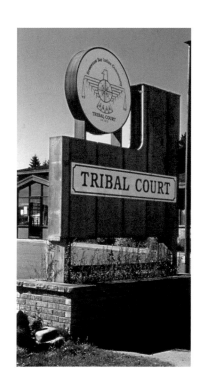

Tribal court building in Baraga, Michigan. Tribal governments have responsibility for law enforcement in many reservation communities.

Chief Justice Marshall elaborated on his vague characterization of the Cherokees as "domestic dependent nations." He stated that the "Indian nations had always been considered as distinct, independent political communities, retaining their original natural rights, as the undisputed possessors of the soil, from time immemorial, with the single exception imposed by irresistible power, which excluded them from intercourse with any other European potentate than the first discoverer of the coast of the particular region claim." Marshall concluded that "a weak state, in order to provide for its safety, may place itself under the protection of a more powerful, without stripping itself of the right of government, and ceasing to be a state." A good deal of subsequent history of conflict between the United States and the Indian tribes has revolved around the question of preserving the right of self-government and the attributes of Indian sovereignty as suggested in Marshall's decision.

Influences of Traditional Leadership on Contemporary Leaders

European colonization had a profound impact on the methods of governance in Ojibwe communities and the means in which leaders were selected and then governed. In some ways, however, the old still influences the new.

The problems of contemporary Indian leadership noted in the story of my brother Sonny and his detractors of "Camp Truth" is an example of the politics of personality and factionalism found in some Ojibwe communities. One of the most comprehensive studies of the problems of contemporary tribal leadership was done by Murray Wax (1971), who noted that many traditional Indian societies were based on moral authority. He concluded that the conditions of everyday reservation life have destroyed the upper levels of intellectual and spiritual leadership. In the past, the community may have been able to draw upon the wisdom and knowledge of elders and other wise persons. As the number of elders who followed traditional lifestyles and beliefs decreased, Wax noted a corresponding decline in the number of traditional leaders. According to Wax, the basis for traditional authority eroded and no system existed for training younger leaders. Additionally, poverty and oppression accentuated the fear of change in these communities. Wax also stated that the attempts of government, churches, foundations, and universities to produce new Indian leaders failed. Many of these "leaders," who left the reservation to be trained and returned years later, are viewed as unworthy of leadership by many reservation Indians. These "leaders" can only assume "leadership" in pan-Indian agencies, such as the

Current Ojibwe reservations

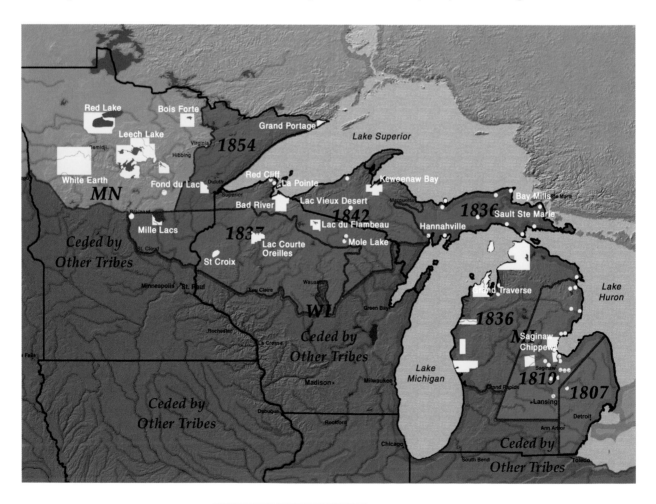

Bureau of Indian Affairs and tribal offices, where their ability to compete in the off-reservation world and act as Indian spokespersons has value. Others may consider these persons to be leaders within these agencies, and the media may think of them as representatives of Indian concerns. They are not, however, accepted as leaders by the traditional Indians of the community.

Ebbott (1985) in describing traditional Ojibwe culture explored the egalitarian ethos and leadership functions based on moral authority. She discussed how the powers of traditional leaders were limited and for some temporary leaders were to be followed only so long as something had to be accomplished. There was no centralized authority system in the great Ojibwe nation. It was the creation of non-Indian economic forces, according to Ebbott, that contributed to the decline of traditional leadership practices.

Further complicating the traditional-contemporary political conflict is a struggle over what limited power exists. With the current emphasis on power politics, individuals and political factions vie for control of tribal councils and the programs and businesses under the councils' jurisdiction. The stakes are high and include authority over who gets jobs, housing, and services; who decides about the spending of casino or other revenue; and who gets to rub elbows with big-wigs in the non-Indian world. In some communities, a winner-takes-all attitude prevails, and a revolving door of "innies" and "outies" is a fact of life, as noted by one Ojibwe politician (Peacock, 1989, p. 53):

Currently, I don't have an official role in tribal government. I used to be somewhat of an innie, but I had outie ideas which kept conflicting with my innie position and station so I had to either resign my position or change my concept about how things should be done. I resigned my job to join the outies. I soon found out that the outies only wanted to become innies and make the current innies outies, so I became a contrary.

Vine Deloria, a noted Lakota author, lamented the change from moral to political leadership in Indian societies and, like many, dreamed of a time when our modern Indian leaders will emulate the great Oglala chief, Crazy Horse (1969):

Crazy Horse never drafted anyone to follow him. People recognized what Crazy Horse did was for the best and was for the people. Crazy Horse never had his name on the stationary. He never had business cards. He never even received a per diem. . . . Until we can produce people like Crazy Horse all the money and help in the world will not save us. It is up to us to write the final chapter of the American Indian on this continent.

Evolution from Traditional to Contemporary Leadership and Governance

Small, independent groups of Ojibwe communities, governed by councils of elders, women and men, and hereditary leaders, functioned well for many thousands of years. The coming of Europeans, however, permanently changed that. Europeans demanded a spokesperson, someone who could represent the masses and make quick decisions about trading and settling disputes with our indigenous neighbors, the Dakota or Fox or Iroquois. Most importantly, the colonists needed

Billboard for gaiashkibos, then a candidate for the Wisconsin state legislature

the spokesperson to negotiate agreements so they could acquire our land and resources. A new type of leader emerged, and hereditary leaders and their second chiefs and warriors became treaty negotiators and signers. People who could speak French, and later English, acted as spokespersons, and therefore leaders, of Ojibwe people. Moreover, Ojibwe people who could engage in the social discourse demanded by Euro-American society (idle chit chat, talking more than listening) were favored over those who were more traditional listeners than speakers. As intermarriage occurred, mixed-blood leaders emerged because of their ability to act as intermediaries between the traditional Ojibwe and non-Indians. Later, when the federal government sanctioned tribal councils to advise Indian agents, many of the councils were made up of mixed bloods, while full bloods formed their own unsanctioned councils. Furthermore, Ojibwe lands were divided and became part of territorial, state, county, and federal jurisdictions, and the people were moved onto reservation lands, where the Indian agent made many of the day-to-day decisions. The Indian agent was just one entity in a long hierarchical line of government bureaucrats, topped by the U.S. president, that came to define the federal-Indian relationship (Ojibwe Curriculum Committee, 1973): president, secretary of the interior, commissioner of Indian affairs, regional superintendent, Indian agent, subagents, interpreters, tribal councils. The old ways of governing and leading were no more.

The deplorable state of many reservation communities in the early part of the twentieth century led to the Merriam Report of 1928 and the Indian Reorganization Act of 1934. In Minnesota, the White Earth, Leech Lake, Fond du Lac, Mille Lacs, Bois Forte, and Grand Portage bands formed the Minnesota Chippewa Tribe. The Red Lake band, which had organized in 1918, chose to remain independent. Other Ojibwe bands forged communities (Ojibwe Curriculum Committee, 1973, p. 46):

Veterans have traditionally been held in high esteem in Ojibwe country. This memorial for Ojibwe veterans is at the Pinery in L'Anse, Michigan.

Ojibwe in Michigan formed three tribal groups. The Sault Ste. Marie band organized separately as the Bay Mills Indian Community, while the L'Anse, Lac Vieux Desert, and Ontonagon bands united as the Keweenaw Bay Indian Community, and the Saginaw, Swan Creek and Black River bands in Lower Michigan incorporated under the Saginaw Chippewa Indian Tribe.

The Red Cliff, Bad River, Lac Court Oreilles, and Lac du Flambeau bands organized separately, as did the western bands. In 1961, many of the Wisconsin bands formed the Great Lakes Intertribal Council. The Chippewa Cree of Montana created the Rocky Boy Reservation, and the Little Shell band of North Dakota became the Turtle Mountain Chippewa Tribe.

Perhaps the most important recent change was the enaction in 1975 of the Indian Self-Determination and Education Assistance Act, which allowed tribes to contract for programs and services previously provided by the Bureau of Indian Affairs and Indian Public Health Service. Since then, tribes have developed and run their own programs, albeit with the restrictions inherent in federal rules and regulations. Schools, health centers, social services, and police and natural resource departments, all tribally run, evolved as a result. No other act has had such a profound impact on the growth and influence of modern tribal governments.

Ojibwe Medicine Leadership

Spiritual leaders can have as much importance in Ojibwe communities as political leaders. Often elders and traditional medicine people provide the moral and spiritual leadership. They supply the teachings, through ceremony and by example, of the values and cultural knowledge that make up the heart of Ojibwe culture. Medicine people are well recognized in Ojibwe communities, and their advice is sought from people in all levels of the community, including tribally elected leaders, on aspects of physical, emotional, psychological, and spiritual well-being. Rosemary Christensen (Mole Lake Ojibwe) has furnished a rare glimpse of the leadership of medicine people. They have a special status, akin to that of religious leaders in Euro-American society. A fundamental difference, however, is that medicine people are the keepers of the ancient teachings, known and practiced by very few. Christensen defined medicine leaders as ones who (1999):

— Translate traditional teachings from elders into group action
— Know and live teachings
— Teach the Spirit Code
— Are inclusive
— Live, work, and act in culturally defined condition
— Possess attributes needed for demanding work: persuade through charisma, have energy, and provide rational arguments for theological positions
— Demonstrate cultural knowledge, act in culturally acceptable ways (independence, respect, use Ojibwe language).

Tom Shingobe, Ojibwe spiritual leader, at his home in Minneapolis, 1978

Modern Ojibwe tribal councils, established as a result of the Indian Reorganization Act of 1934, are elected, representative democracies. The include (Jaakola, 1999):

— **Bois Forte:** established by Treaty of April 1866 and Executive Order of December 1881; has five-person council consisting of a chairperson, secretary-treasurer, and district representatives

— **Fond du Lac (Nahgahchiwanong):** established by Treaty of 1854; has a five-person council consisting of a chairperson, secretary-treasurer, and district representatives

— **Grand Portage:** established by Treaty of 1854; has a five-person council consisting of chairperson, secretary-treasurer, and committee members

— **Leech Lake:** established by Treaties of 1855, 1863, and 1867 and Executive Orders of 1873 and 1874; has a five-person council consisting of a chairperson, secretary-treasurer, and district representatives

— **Mille Lacs:** established by Treaty of 1855; has a five-person council consisting of a chief executive, secretary-treasurer, and district representatives

— **Red Lake (Mishkwagamiwizagaiganing):** established by Treaties of 1863 and 1864 and the Act of 1889; has an eleven-person council consisting of a chairperson, secretary, treasurer, and two district representatives each from the communities of Little Rock, Redby, Red Lake, and Ponemah

— **White Earth:** established by Treaty of 1867; has a council consisting of a chairperson, secretary-treasurer, and district representatives

— **Bad River (Mashkiziibii):** established by Treaty of 1854; has a council consisting of chairperson, vice-chairperson, secretary, treasurer, and three other members (Bad River was founded by Babomnigoniboy (Spreading Eagle) of the Loon clan, who brought his family from Madeline Island; these were mostly families who converted to Protestantism)

— **Lac Courte Oreilles (Ottawasawasii'igii'igoning):** established by Treaty of 1854; has a council consisting of a chairperson, vice-chairperson, secretary-treasurer, and four other members (the area was settled by three brothers of the Bear clan who left Madeline Island)

— **Lac du Flambeau (Waswagoning):** established by Treaty of 1854; has a council consisting of a president, vice-president, secretary, treasurer, and eight other members (community was initially settled by Crane clan people, led by Kishkimun)

— **Red Cliff (Gitigoning):** established by Treaty of 1854; has a council consisting of a chairperson, vice-chairperson, secretary, treasurer, and five other members (the first Ojibwe residents at Buffalo Bay, later changed to Red Cliff, were descendants of converted Catholics from Madeline Island, and many of them were Loon clan people)

— **Mole Lake (Sokoagon):** established by proclamation of the secretary of interior; has a council consisting of a chairperson, vice-chairperson, secretary, treasurer, and two other members (the area was initially settled when Chief Kijiwabesheshi left Madeline Island to live near Crandon, Wisconsin; the treaty of 1847 reserved a mere twelve acres for the Skoagon band, and it was not until 1934 that the reservation was recognized by the federal government)

— **St. Croix:** established by proclamation of the secretary of interior in 1938; has a council consisting of a president, vice-president, secretary-treasurer, and two other members (initially settled by Ojibwe of the Marten clan who left Madeline Island and settled along the St. Croix River)

— **Bay Mills:** established by the Act of 1860; has a council consisting of president, vice-president, secretary, treasurer, and another member

— **Grand Traverse:** established by proclamation of the secretary of the interior in 1984; has a council consisting of a chairperson, vice chairperson, secretary, treasurer, and three other councilors

— **Keweenaw Bay:** established by Treaty of 1854; has a council consisting of president, vice-president, secretary, assistant secretary, treasurer, and seven other members

— **Lac View Desert:** established by Public Law 100-240 in 1988; has a council consisting of a chairperson, vice-chairperson, secretary, treasurer, and five other members

— **Saginaw Bay:** established by Treaty of 1864; has a council consisting of a chief, subchief, secretary, treasurer, and eight other members

— **Sault Ste. Marie:** established by proclamation of the secretary of the interior in 1974; has a council consisting of a chairperson, vice-chairperson, secretary, treasurer, and nine other unit members.

Walt Bresette

Contemporary Leaders

This is a difficult topic given the fragmented nature by which we as Ojibwe people sometimes define "leaders." Ideally, we should accept as leaders people from all arenas of Ojibwe life, including medicine people, elders, politicians, educators, human service providers, legal authorities, authors, artists, and others. Moreover, leaders are at all levels of the community. Some are leaders only in their small, respective communities; others are recognized in national or state circles. Political leaders such as gaiashkibos (former chairman of Lac Courte Oreilles), Roger Jourdain (former chairman of the Red Lake Nation), and Marge Anderson (former chairman of Mille Lacs) have a national reputation in tribal government circles. Educators such as Rosemary Christensen (Mole Lake), Rick St. Germaine (Lac Courte Oreilles) and David Beaulieu (White Earth) travel in national Indian educator circles. Ojibwe authors, including Louise Erdrich (Turtle Mountain) Gerald Vizenor (White Earth), Winona LaDuke (White Earth), and Jim Northrup (Fond du Lac), have a national readership. George Morrison's (Grand Portage) and Patrick DeJarlait's (Red Lake) art work are displayed in international art circles. Walt Bresette (Red Cliff) was a well-known environmentalist.

We look upon some people as leaders who help others in our communities, but are not as visible. These leaders visit elders and give them bread, jam, deer meat, rabbits, and fish. They take in children who need homes. They cook and serve meals when there are funerals in our communities. They share their knowledge of traditional things without want of an honorarium or per diem. They lead in quiet ways. And when they are gone from this earth, they leave a space that cannot be filled.

Winona LaDuke, author and White Earth band member, was a Green Party candidate for vice president of the United States in 2000.

Tribes of the Twenty-first Century

Deloria and Lytle (1984) provided a framework for looking at the potential of tribal governance and leaders. Some of their ideas have already been adopted:

— Development of national tribal governments. An Ojibwe nation may emerge to represent all bands of the Ojibwe people in the United States and, possibly, Canada.

— Separation of executive, legislative, and judicial functions. In some bands, the tribal council enacts, manages, and enforces its laws with no balance of power. This system is subject to the misuse of power.

— Larger tribal councils that are more representative and create a closer relationship between leaders and the community. Form local councils with limited jurisdiction. This would create governance similar to that of more traditional times when councils existed in each community.

— Use of tribal customs in judging cases brought to tribal court. For example, the Ojibwe notion of reciprocity could be used to handle disputes between individuals. Moreover, a council of elders may be better than tribal courts at handling domestic disputes.

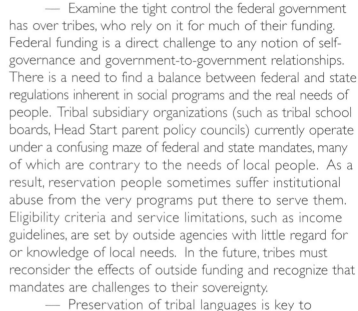

— Examine the tight control the federal government has over tribes, who rely on it for much of their funding. Federal funding is a direct challenge to any notion of self-governance and government-to-government relationships. There is a need to find a balance between federal and state regulations inherent in social programs and the real needs of people. Tribal subsidiary organizations (such as tribal school boards, Head Start parent policy councils) currently operate under a confusing maze of federal and state mandates, many of which are contrary to the needs of local people. As a result, reservation people sometimes suffer institutional abuse from the very programs put there to serve them. Eligibility criteria and service limitations, such as income guidelines, are set by outside agencies with little regard for or knowledge of local needs. In the future, tribes must reconsider the effects of outside funding and recognize that mandates are challenges to their sovereignty.

— Preservation of tribal languages is key to cultural renewal and survival and must be "the substance of self-determination" (Deloria and Lytle, 1984, p. 251). "The cultural revival and integrity of the American Indian community depends on the cultivation of a responsible

Some Ojibwe people lead in quiet ways by visiting elders and giving them bread, jam, deer meat, rabbits, and fish.

attitude and behavior patterns in the communities themselves" (Deloria and Lytle, 1984, p. 254). The preservation of the Ojibwe language is a community responsibility that must be accepted by the tribal governments, schools, and families. Successful tribal language revitalization programs exist in Maori (New Zealand) and Hawaiian communities. Perhaps the best example of language renewal is in the nation of Israel, where Hebrew, a language in decline, was reclaimed to be the language of government, commerce, and culture.

— Economic stability is key to preserving what limited sovereignty tribes now enjoy. Good jobs and a flourishing economy do more to solve the social ills of a community than any social program could ever do. Given the pressure by states to limit the ability of tribes to be self-governing, casino tribes will struggle to maintain their freedom to have casino gambling as a resource. Furthermore, they will have to diversify in order to prepare for a future that is not dependent on casino revenue.

Summary

THERE SEEM TO BE two arenas where the Ojibwe leadership will be severely tested. One arena is internal, and the issues raised by Deloria and Lytle, together with the story of my brother Sonny's struggle with his detractors, highlight the intensity of that struggle. The other arena is external, coming both from the challenges of state and federal governments to our sovereignty and the interrelated complexity of institutional racism as a whole.

I often see flaws in the American democracy, in part because I see how subjective it is, how it tends to favor the elite, and how it is often used to challenge the limited sovereignty of tribes. My reservation neighbors have not benefited as well from our nation's free form of capitalism as town people have. Several years ago, when the tribal council members decided to become good capitalists and opened several casinos, they had to battle area restaurant and motel owners, who pleaded to the state and federal government about Indians having an "unfair advantage" in the casino industry. We continue to argue and negotiate with state governments to retain our right to offer casino jobs and to spend the funds casinos generate for services in our communities. We have spent millions of dollars in litigation costs as a result of lawsuits by state governments over the hunting and fishing rights guaranteed to us in treaties. Moreover, we are not well represented in local units of government, nor in the informal power structures found in the non-Indian world. Ojibwe people are under-represented or not represented at all on the boards of directors of local banks, although millions of dollars of tribal revenue flow through those very banks. Few of our people sit on local school boards, although these are the very schools where our children struggle and where our history and culture and ways of being are either not taught at all or are taught only because of the presence of special "Indian money." Few of us are members of the tight fabric of the non-Indian power world — the local Kiwanis, Rotary clubs, chambers of commerce, historical societies, or private golf courses built on land taken from our ancestors. So I am one who challenges the way in which the Founding Fathers, as well their descendants, took a uniquely American Indian form of democracy and fashioned it to favor those of European extraction.

On a more fundamental level, we carry in us the capacity both for greatness and for our own destruction. My brother Sonny's struggle with his political adversaries of "Camp Truth" is symbolic of our knack for self-ruination. This self-destruction received attention from the non-Indian media, which seemed to love seeing Indians fight among themselves, and we seemed to enjoy displaying our differences on the nightly news. That struggle wasn't a simple disagreement between have's or have nots, "innies" or "outies," neo-traditional pan-Indians or assimilated mixed bloods, or anything that well defined. It was a complex dance of competition for scarce resources (power), of cultural beliefs, and of socioeconomic reality. It was us confronting our greatest enemy — Ourselves.

When I was young and would fight with my older brothers, our grandfather would pull us aside and say, "You boys quit your fighting now." And we would quit because our grandfather told us to. Mostly we didn't have time to fight. There was too much to do. There were catfish lines to set and catfish to skin and eat and sell. There was wild rice to harvest and finish and sell for money for school clothes. There were berries to pick and sell for basic essentials. There were rabbit snares to check so we could give fresh rabbit to our grandmother. And there was firewood to cut and stack for winter.

There are lessons in that. Mi-I-iw.

Gus Lemieux, a Fond du Lac elder and descendent of Osaugee, a leader at Fond du Lac, was the oldest member of the band and the oldest World War I veteran in Wisconsin until his death in December 1999.

WIIGWAASIJIIMAANIKEWAG
(they are building a birch-bark canoe)

Canoes, a primary means of transportation in early times, were still being built in the traditional way in 1895.

Gaa-miinigooyang
That Which is Given To Us

MANY OJIBWE FAMILIES were poor back in the early 1950s when I was growing up, and they survived any way they could. In my family, all of us contributed, even the kids. My grandmother cleaned the homes of wealthy townspeople, and on Saturdays she cleaned the Northern Printery in Cloquet, Minnesota. I remember going there with her on many occasions under the guise of being a helper. Mostly I wanted to spend time with her, and I ended up just getting in her way as she worked. My grandfather was an itinerant golf-ball hunter, who sold golf balls to paper mill executives. He sometimes used his proceeds to buy cheap wine at Vnuk's Liquor Store, which he drank under the shade of trees in the pasture that I now call my own and also in a place called Bottle Alley (because that was what it was). I remember how he had to endure the indignity of being called "Chief" by the non-Indians he sold golf balls to. He would look at the ground when he was addressed that way. He had his pride.

To an outside observer, it would seem my family was welfare trash. I grew fat on government commodities and became resentful of the social workers who would come into our home and tell us how we should live our lives. We, however, worked hard for life's necessities. In summer we peeled pulp wood with our father, who sold it to buy cigarettes and bologna and sometimes old Indian cars or to go on an occasional drinking binge. We also picked blueberries and sold them by the crate to Jaskari's Store in Sawyer, and we picked potatoes for a local farmer, and we caught and sold catfish to our neighbors. In fall we harvested wild rice and sold it to buy school clothes. In winter we snared rabbits and trapped weasels. We sold the rabbits for their meat and the weasels for the bounty paid by the state warden's office. In spring we waited for summer, when the whole cycle would begin all over again.

Many families from the reservation survived in a similar manner. A few families worked at the Indian hospital, including Lizzy (Bear) Smith, Ben Bassett, Izzy Savage (Whelan), and a few others. To be sure, there were also some who worked good jobs in town. Aubie Gurno and Jay Smith worked in the local wood mill, and we would see them every work day as they trekked to and from town, walking the tracks or the old tote roads, their lunch pails swinging as they walked by. A few of the town Indians worked in the local paper mill and the match factory. They were, however, town Indians, and back then most of them

ODADAAWAAGENAAW
AA MIINAN
(they sell blueberries)

Until a few years ago, many Ojibwe children worked to contribute to the economic well-being of the family, like these children selling blueberries in 1912.

NANDAWENJIGEWIN
(to get food by hunting or
gathering)

Moose hunt at Grand Portage

wouldn't even admit they were Indian. Today I am not resentful of them because they suddenly discovered they were Indians when it became chic, and their children and grandchildren now hold many of the high-paying jobs in the reservation bureaucracy. The town Indians did what they could to survive, even if it meant denying their Ojibwe heritage.

My family lived in other people's abandoned houses. One of my earliest memories was living in the old Murray farm, which had a second floor so rotten we couldn't use it for fear we would fall through. We then moved into the Savages' house after they moved to Canada, but we had to abandon it when they moved back to the reservation. So we moved into the Shotley family's old house, which was a tar-paper shack in the middle of the field where our sparkling new tribal center now stands. Then, suddenly, we were rich (at least from my perspective). My mother, who was by then a nurse's aide at the Indian hospital, bought the old doctor's quarters, which had stood abandoned with broken windows in an uncut field, for three hundred dollars. So for the next ten years we lived in a house with new glass windows on the first floor and flapping plastic windows on the second floor because we couldn't afford to buy all that glass.

We lived there until the reservation built its first housing project, and we moved into a sparkling new three-bedroom, government-green HUD rambler. There we became disgustingly lower middle class because my father was lucky enough to land a job as a janitor at the hospital in town.

I miss the simplicity of those times, but only temporarily because I also remember the grinding poverty and the sense that there was no way out, what Chester Pierce, one of my college professors, called "perfect pain."

A Chapter Road Map

FROM THE 1950s TO TODAY, I have seen the economic transition of Ojibwe people as we have moved from the economic ways of our traditional hunter-gatherer-agriculturist society to lives of social-welfare dependency and then to the contemporary self-reliant government and business economy. This chapter covers each of those distinct historical periods. It begins by describing survival and the traditional Ojibwe economy before contact with Europeans, that great span of time when the Ojibwe were hunters-gatherers-agriculturists. It then moves into the period dominated by the fur trade, and its economic impact on the Ojibwe. (A description of the period of exploitation of the mineral and timber resources in Ojibwe country with the devastating impact of that period on the environment, as well as the people, is covered in another section.) It covers the stark reality of the federal paternalistic economy, when many Ojibwe people were dependent upon the government for their day-to-day survival. It discusses governmental attempts to turn us Ojibwe into farmers. Contemporary Ojibwe society, including tribally owned and managed businesses, is described. Finally, it considers the combined impact these historical periods may have on the future, where our grandchildren and great-grandchildren will not have to endure the social and economic dysfunction experienced by generations of their ancestors and where they will become a people strong in their ways, still hopeful and living purposeful lives.

Ojibwe women selling 60 pound packs of maple sugar in birch-bark containers, ca. 1910. The sale of Ojibwe-produced goods provided supplemental income in many families.

Ways of the Grandfathers

We will never fully know the story of our ancestors' survival on this land. Most of our stories only go back to the recent ice age, the time of the Grandfathers, the Lenni Lenape. Their ways of living on this land were similar to those of our recent ancestors, reflecting a traditional hunter-gatherer-agriculturist economy that revolved around the seasons. The earliest recollection of our ancestors was told in the Wallum Olum (McCutchen, 1993, p. 31):

Among the Lenni Lenape, there was a customary division of labor between men and women, but the division was not unequal, and each would lend a hand as needed. Women were not expected to be councilors, but they owned most of the household property and the products of the fields they tended. Men were responsible for clearing the fields and hunting for meat in the forests. Children were loved and valued, and everyone in the village gladly lent a hand in bringing them up to be a part of the community. Elders were universally respected for their wisdom and experience, and every grey hair was considered a badge of honor. Life revolved around the cycle of seasons, as reflected in the changes in the Lenni

Lenape's woodland home. When spring came, the Lenni Lenape congregated by rapids and waterfalls to gather the spawning fish swarming upstream, hunt bear and deer, and pick strawberries. As summer approached, the people dispersed; some went to the seashore to gather shellfish for food and for shells used in making valuable wampum beads. Most went inland to prepare their garden plots in the soft, deep soil of the river bottoms, clearing fields by charring trees in order to fell them with stone axes, then planting crops of corn, beans, squash, and tobacco in the ash-enriched soil. Summer was the time for tending plots, gathering fruits, berries, and medicinal herbs, hunting and fishing, and taking trips to trade, explore, and visit relatives. Autumn was the time for group hunts, using fire to drive the game and to clear the brush under the trees, and for gathering and storing the harvest. In the winter, warm in their fur robes inside their wigwams and bark houses, they would listen to stories and create cloths, weapons, and household items with skill and artistry.

As our Anishinabe ancestors began their westward journey as one people with the Ottawa and Pottawatomi, they adapted their ways of living and surviving to the changing geography of the area. Ebbott (1985, p. 19) noted how these adaptions were made:

BAWA'IANG
(she knocks it off)

Alice Cadotte knocking wild rice at Lac Courte Oreilles, 1941. Until recently, wild rice was a prime source of both income and food in many Ojibwe communities.

Both the Dakota and Ojibway adapted their economics to the resources and limitations of the Minnesota country. They hunted and fished; gathered wild rice, berries, and maple syrup; built houses of poles and skins or bark in semipermanent villages; traveled in summer by birchbark canoes along the countless waterways and in winter on snowshoes.

During the time when the entire people of the southern Ojibwe nation were living on Madeline Island, the economy was primarily one of fishing, hunting, and agriculture. These ways of being lasted for many generations (Warren, 1984, p. 97):

While hemmed in on this island by their enemies, the Ojibways lived mainly by fishing. They also practised the arts of agriculture to an extent not since known amongst them. Their gardens are said to have been extensive, and they raised large quantities of Mun-dam-in (Indian corn), and pumpkins.

WANIIÍGEWININI
(trapper)

Muskrat trapper at Lac Courte Orielles, 1941. Hunting, fishing, and trapping were of great importance in providing food and income in earlier times.

The more hardy and adventurous hunted on the lake shore opposite their village, which was overrun with moose, bear, elk and deer. The buffalo, also, are said in those days to have ranged within a half day's march from the lake shore, on the barrens stretching towards the headwaters of the St. Croix River. Every stream which emptied into the lake, abounded with beaver, otter, and muskrat, and the fish which swam in its clear water could not be surpassed in quality or quantity in any other spot on earth.

To be sure, traditional Ojibwe people worked in many occupations. Most people were generalists, laboring in a variety of ways to contribute to the well-being of the community: medicine people, hunters, fishermen, agriculturists, warriors, orators, leaders, and midwives (gata niwi kwe). Others became skilled craftspeople: canoe makers, bow and arrow makers, builders of snowshoes and toboggans, net makers, net menders, makers of containers and mats, dwelling makers, and people skilled in the preparation and storage of food. One of Hilger's Vermilion informants recalled learning the art of canoe making and lamented that young people no longer wanted to learn the craft (1992, p. 117):

As a young lad I had often watched my father make canoes and in that way learnt how to do the fine details. My father was considered an expert canoe maker: he had learnt it from his father who also had a reputation for canoe making. I made my first one when I was 14 years old; an old woman directed me and showed me exactly how to put the parts together. It was the same size as this one; 14 feet 2 inches long, 38 inches wide, and about 18 inches deep. No one today wants to help me, nor learn. These boys you see around here watch 10 minutes and then run away.

The Fur Trade Economy

The arrival of Europeans had a profound effect on the amount and nature of trading between the Ojibwe and other groups. To be sure, there was extensive trading among the Ojibwe and their tribal neighbors; however, it was nothing compared to the level and intensity of what would develop with the French, English, and Americans. Our Ojibwe ancestors valued the material goods of the colonizers over those the people had used for many thousands of years. Shown below are some examples of the value of trade goods for beaver pelts used by the Hudson's Bay Trading Company (Ray, 1974, p. 66-67):

Goods	1720-21	1760-61
Kettles	1 1/2 per lb.	————
Gun Powder	1 per lb.	1 per lb.
Shot	1 per 4 lbs.	1 per 4 lbs.
Tobacco	2 per lb.	1 per 3/4 lb.
Beads(large)	4 per lb.	————
Guns	14 each	14 each
Hatchets	1 per 1	1 per 1
Blankets	7 per 1	7 per 1
Cloth (broad)	3 per yard	————
Brandy	4 per gal.	4 per gal.
Knives	————	1 per 4

The value of trade was not simply in goods; it was also in the forming of unequal alliances and the subsequent dependency of the Ojibwe on the French and later on the English and American traders. One way for traders to ensure this dependency was to extend credit, particularly to Ojibwe leaders, who in turn might influence band members to trade with specific individuals and the companies they represented (Ray, 1974, p. 137–138):

In their attempts to assure themselves of a portion of the returns of future Indian hunts, the various European trading groups gave the Indians sizable advances of goods, particularly in the autumn and to a lesser extent in the spring, hoping that they would be able to collect these debts the following season.

The most valuable possession of the European colonizers, however, was the firearm, and with it the Ojibwe reigned over other tribal nations, using it to drive the Dakota, Fox, and Menominee from what is today Ojibwe country.

The French were the first to build trading posts in the Lake Superior region. The first posts included the forts at Grand Portage (Ke-che-o-ne-gum-eng) and on the Island of LaPointe, or Madeline Island (Warren, 1984). Beaver were plentiful throughout the region, and their hides were prized throughout Europe for their exquisite beauty, softness, and density. When the supply of beaver was near exhaustion, the trade in marten and muskrat furs increased, until they too were depleted. Fisher, lynx, otter, and mink were also valuable. By the 1870s, the fur trade was essentially over (Ray, 1974), and the Ojibwe people began years of reliance on the federal government for survival.

The Loss of Timber and Mineral Resources: A Long Period of Dependency

As the fur trade era ended, companies endeavored to get the rich timber and mineral resources on Indian land. The efforts to transform and "civilize" the Ojibwe, and to take our land under the guise of helping us, took several forms: cutting timber and extracting minerals from reservation lands; attempting to turn Ojibwe people into farmers; developing a federal paternalistic economy in which the Ojibwe people became dependent upon rations and governmental assistance for day-to-day survival. All of these policies proved to be destructive of the physical and psychological well-being of Ojibwe people.

The Taking of Ojibwe Timber and Mineral Resources

After resettling Ojibwe on reservations, the colonizers should have satisfied their almost insatiable hunger for land. Yet it was not to be. The General Allotment Act (Dawes Act) of 1887 allocated up to 160 acres to individual Indians within the confines of reservations, while the remainder of the land was to be sold to whites so they could access the huge timber and mineral reserves. What happened was part of the ongoing tragedy that has marked the history between Ojibwe people and Euro-Americans, as exemplified by the taking of White Earth lands (Ojibwe Curriculum Committee, 1973, p. 36):

There were other ways in which Ojibwe land was lost. Mineral seekers convinced the federal government to use treaties to acquire large sections of land in Upper Michigan and northern Minnesota, which they developed into copper and iron mines.

Through a long series of unfair state laws [Nelson Act of 1889], and through every form of fraud and trickery "that human ingenuity could devise," according to one United States inspector, the White Earth Ojibwe were stripped of their land. By 1909 — only twenty years after allotment — 80 percent of the reservation had passed into private hands, and Indian people had received no more than a tenth of its value. The once prosperous Ojibwe community had been reduced to the grimmest poverty. According to the nationally respected anthropologist Ales Hrdlicka, White Earth had become "one of the most shameful pages in the history of the white man's dealings with the Indian."

The story of what happened at White Earth was repeated all over Ojibwe country. Timber from the land was sometimes taken without the consent of the people. "Dead and down" permits issued to Indian people were bought up by timber barons, and whole sections of land, including standing timber, were clear-cut. Moreover, bid sales of Ojibwe timber property were often sold far below actual value.

Like the vast white pine forests that once dominated the landscape of the Ojibwe nation, the mineral resources were also taken. The great copper and iron reserves of Michigan fell to mining interests, as did the world's richest iron reserves, which were located in northern Minnesota. On the Fond du Lac Reservation, the family of Nord Albert Posey (a blacksmith who had married an Ojibwe woman) was murdered because he would not reveal the whereabouts of the iron ore delivered to him by his Ojibwe friends. Posey's house was burned; he and his two children died (Peacock, 1998):

A woman jerking venison, a traditional way of preserving meat, at Lac Courte Orielles, 1941

The gold rush of the 1860s in northern Minnesota brought prospectors, among them George R. Stuntz, early resident and surveyor. The Chippewa brought rock to Posey from the Vermilion area to ask if it was gold, and

A demonstration of muskie spearing equipment, Lac Courte Orielles, 1949

recognizing hematite iron Posey brought samples to Stuntz and Lewis Merritt, of the mining family, in 1863, but neither was very interested at the time.

In 1865, Stuntz took samples of the rich ore of the Vermilion to Duluth for "tests that proved the commercial value of what later was called the Lee and Breitung mines and Stuntz stated later that the first white man to know that iron [ore] existed on the Vermilion Range was a man named N. A. Posey."

Stuntz told no one until 1874, and then George Stone went with the information to Charlemagne Tower, a mining investor, who sent a crew in 1875, with Stuntz as a guide, to check the Vermilion area. Geologist Arthur Chester described that his part of the exploring party went first by rail to the Northern Pacific Junction, and across the portage to Posey's, where they obtained two large canoes. "As we left Joe Posey's house, we left behind us the last signs of civilization on the St. Louis River, and we hailed it again with satisfaction on our return. . . . [Posey's] wife was a good cook and housekeeper, and we could always get a square meal and a good bed."

The Legislature, in 1875, granted lands to the Duluth and Iron Range Railroad Company, later acquired by the Duluth & Winnipeg Railroad and Stuntz completed his last exploration for ore at Vermilion for Tower and Associates in 1881.

During this time, Posey was threatened by two men who came to his house demanding to know where the ore samples he had shown to Stuntz had been found, and at his refusal to tell, they said they would be back.

Ojibwe Farmers

The Dawes Act was supposed, through individual allotments, to allow Indians to farm the land. Government farms popped up everywhere in Ojibwe country, and the Indian and the government farmer often became one and the same person. Educational programs to train Indians in Euro-American agricultural practices were implemented on a massive scale, programs that were financed by the sale of surplus Ojibwe lands (Ebbott, 1985). It failed. For the most part, Ojibwe people did not make good farmers. Government farms and the farmers hired to "civilize" the Ojibwe people went the way of the horse and buggy.

On my reservation, the government farm stood abandoned when I was a young boy, but it was eventually occupied by my Ojibwe neighbors in need of a house to call a home: the Jacksons, Martineaus, and, finally, the Divers. I remember jumping around in piles of abandoned hay in the abandoned barn. I remember watching as it was torn down. We used it for kindling wood. The Ojibwe may not be good farmers, but we are a resourceful people.

Rossel William tending his garden, 1941

This Ojibwe artisan at Lac du Flambeau in 1908 was one of many who sold crafts to tourists, an important source of income.

A Long Period of Dependency

After the extortion of the remaining Ojibwe lands, the depletion of the fur-bearing animals, the exploitation of timber and mineral resources on Indian lands, and the failed efforts at turning the people into farmers came a long period of dependency upon government food rations, or commodities. The threat of withholding rations was used to force parents to send their children to boarding school and to get our leaders to sign treaties. And this period of dependency continued from the time the first bag of flour was unloaded off the back of a wagon until recent times, when a declining minority of Ojibwe people remain dependent on welfare. The devastation this has wrought on our collective self-consciousness is immeasurable (Ebbott, 1985, p. 47):

Indians are the only race in the United States that has experienced the deliberate, official government effort to wipe out its way of life, language, and culture. They were conquered, colonized, and subjected to social engineering, culture shock, relocation, and forced negative education. Indians retain very little trust of the white system. As they face the questions of who they are and what the system has done to them, they react in a variety of ways.

For some the response is violence. Anger may be turned inward, resulting in self-destructive acts, suicide, interfamily problems, poor achievement in school, or chemical dependency. Others feel that because of past wrongs the government owes them a living. Some develop a distrust of non-Indians in any relationship and a heightened sensitivity to disrespect or conflict from whites.

Many Indians have to endure the destructiveness of poverty, in which a person's main concern is survival on the most minimal level. The need to rely on welfare assistance can foster dependency and discourage initiative. Being continually directed by others helps to destroy a person's image of self worth.

The Evolution into a New Ojibwe Economy

Elizabeth Ebbott's *Indians of Minnesota* (1985) painted a dreary picture of employment of Minnesota Indians just a few years ago. The dismal statistics were given a human face when she quoted an interview from a 1979 *St. Paul Pioneer Press* article about Vernon Bellecourt, former secretary-treasurer of the White Earth Reservation and American Indian Movement activist (Ebbott, 1985, p. 108):

Most people can't conceive of what our unemployment is like. It just doesn't seem real to them. Whites look at the numbers, and they think they must be wrong. Their parents tell them about the Depression, and what they don't know is that our unemployment is worse now than the Depression ever was for whites.

The unemployment rates less than twenty years ago approached third-world conditions in many of our communities, ranging from a high of 82 percent (White Earth) to a low of 41 percent (Fond du Lac), according to Ebbott. Statistics in Wisconsin and Michigan Ojibwe communities were similar.

Ojibwe employees at the boat works at Mille Lacs, 1931

Many of our communities had few opportunities for work until a few years ago. It took World War II to open up the world for many young Ojibwe men, who joined the armed forces and fought and died for a country that did not even consider them full-fledged citizens. Vestiges of the Ojibwe people's armed services duties are present today, and a visit to many homes will show pictures of grandparents, parents, and sons and daughters in full military dress proudly displayed in living rooms. One might wonder how it was that Ojibwe people could be so patriotic, but my sense is that it had to do with our warrior past. I shared a recollection of a veteran's pow-wow on my reservation in *Collected Wisdom* (1998):

Those who know the history of the colonization of America might think it was odd that American Indian people would be honoring soldiers who had served in the same military forces that had marched through and dominated their ancestors' tribal nations. A similar American flag to the one that flew over the pow-wow grounds also flew during the U.S. Army's massacre of American Indian men, women and children at Wounded Knee, South Dakota. A similar American flag was flown when thousands of Cherokee were force marched to Oklahoma Territory, a journey that claimed thousands of American Indian lives.

An Ojibwe woman holding a bag of wild rice produced by the Chippewa Indian Co-op Marketing Association in Cass Lake, 1930

As I looked around the pow-wow grounds I saw many of the relatives of these veterans: brothers and sisters, cousins, spouses, parents and grandparents, aunties and uncles, children and grandchildren. As with most pow-wows there were very few non-Indians present. As each name was read and the veteran stepped forward, sections of people in the stands would burst into applause. I noticed many in the crowd were having difficulty maintaining their composure as their hands would go to their mouths as expressions of their emotions.

Most of us were at the pow-wow that day to honor our veterans, our warriors. The Ojibwe people have been doing just that for many thousands of years. We weren't necessarily there to honor war and its madness, including the millions of Vietnamese civilian casualties. Our American Indian ancestors had experienced many of the same atrocities suffered by the Vietnamese. We were there to honor our veterans' safe return, after all these years, because standing in front of us were warriors who had survived the horrors of that war with their bodies still intact, and for most, their sense of being at peace.

The limited opportunities for Ojibwe men continued well through the Vietnam War, but in many respects World War II marked the first great exodus from the reservations. Also during World War II, Ojibwe women found work in off-reservation factories. My mother was one who worked in the local wood mill throughout the war, until the men returned home and reclaimed their jobs.

The span of time between World War II and the 1960s was marked by a second exodus from our reservations as the government's relocation program sent thousands of Ojibwe families to urban areas in Oakland-San Francisco, Minneapolis, Seattle, Chicago, and Cleveland. Many people stayed there, and their children and grandchildren remain part of a large body of Ojibwe people living in Midwest cities, where they have become an integral part of the social and political fabric of pan-Indian urban cultures. Other people spent a few lonely months or years in the cities, only to return home to the land of their birth, to the lakes, woods, and sacred places of their ancestors. There was a joke that made its rounds throughout Ojibwe country during that time: "One sure way to get a man to the moon and back was to send an Indian there on relocation."

People lined up to receive government checks in Minneapolis, January 1, 1931

147 GAA-MIINIGOOYANG

Maddy Moose pours maple sugar into tins to cool and harden into sugar cakes at Heart of the Earth Survival School sugar bush camp, 1984.

The Great Society brought the first major social programs to many reservations. What made these different from other efforts was that they were administered by Indian people. Jobs created as part of youth, elderly, housing, education, and social-service programs led to the development of large tribal infrastructures and to the growing influence of tribal governments. During this period, Ojibwe people began to return to their home to find employment. People competed for a limited number of jobs in tribal and federal bureaucracies (Bureau of Indian Affairs and Indian Public Health Service). In addition, state and federal agencies funded many of the educational, health, and social-service programs and mandated educational and other qualifications that few reservation Indians could meet, which forced many reservations to hire non-Indians in the few prestigious, high-paying jobs. This led to resentment by Indian people in some communities toward the very programs designed to serve them. To complicate matters, few

Indians worked in area factories because of the marked racism in towns near reservations, the lack of skills of many Indian adults, and a variety of other reasons.

The passage of the Indian Regulatory Gaming Act of 1988, and the jobs that resulted, has markedly changed the economies, as well as the social and cultural fabric, of some Ojibwe communities according to a recent social and cultural study of the impact of gaming on a small Great Lakes reservation (Peacock, Day, and Peacock, 1999, p. 28):

The increase in jobs and money associated with gaming was rebuilding both individual and community identities, both of which have suffered from poverty, despair, and accompanying social ills.

By far the most positive impact that gaming has provided is much needed employment on the reservation, and nothing works better to improve both the collective consciousness and individual self-worth than steady employment and a livable wage.

Some Ojibwe communities are now boasting about full employment, have greatly reduced dependency on social-welfare programs for residents, have numerous job opportunities for non-Indians, and have a growing political influence in nearby non-Indian towns. There are, however, some communities that have not profited as much, or at all, by casino gambling, and unemployment rates and the accompanying social ills continue to plague Indian country.

There are many recent efforts at developing reservation owned or managed businesses in Ojibwe communities (Jaakola, 1999). This list is in no way complete, and given the fluid nature of business operations, changes occur often:

— Bois Forte: casino/resort, wild rice production, construction company, sawmill, tribal hunting-guiding services

— Fond du Lac: two casinos (one on the reservation and one in Duluth), construction company, hotel, restaurant

— Grand Portage: casino/lodge, marina, ferry service

Soaring Eagle Casino and Resort in Saginaw, Michigan. "All the decoration of the facility is based on traditional Ojibwe patterns. A landmark of Ojibwe architecture."
—Lyz Jaakola

Inside Soaring Eagle Casino

— Leech Lake: three casinos, a marina, gas station/gift store and restaurant

— Mille Lacs: two casinos, bank, museum

— Red Lake: casino, construction company, fisheries, wild rice production

— White Earth: casino-hotel

— Bad River: casino, logging operation, fish hatchery, convenience store/gas station/mini-casino

— Lac Courte Oreilles: casino, cranberry farm, sawmill, radio station, grocery store, convenience store/gas station

— Lac du Flambeau: casino, fish hatchery, electric company, wood and pallet operation, museum, campground/marina-bait shop, cigarette operations, mall/grocery, gas station

— Red Cliff: casino, fish company, campground/marina complex.

— Sokoagon (Mole Lake): two casinos

— St. Croix: casino, restaurant, construction company, salmon enterprise, computer remanufacturing, convenience store, hotel

— Bay Mills: two casinos, convenience store

— Keweenaw Bay: casino, bowling, restaurant/gift shop, motel, construction company

— Sault Ste. Marie: day-care center, health alliance, casinos, inns, ice arena, apartments, fisheries, art gallery, construction, aviation, sales and rental, car dealership.

Ojibwe reservations are using their casino revenues to establish community infrastructures, as shown by some of the following examples. Among other major projects, the Mille Lacs Band of Ojibwe has built two schools, a tribal complex, a museum, streets, and water and sewer services on its small northern Minnesota reservation. Fond du Lac has erected a new Head Start building and middle school, contributed heavily to a new museum-veterans' cultural center, and constructed community centers-tribal complexes. Grand Portage has constructed a community center complex and new school.

While the jobs and development of community infrastructure created by casino gambling have had a positive impact on Ojibwe communities, there have been some drawbacks (Peacock, Day, and Peacock, 1999, p. 27-28):

There was little middle ground in the perceptions informants had toward gaming's impact on the social and cultural aspects of tribal life. Those who viewed the effects as negative focused on: a perception that gambling was replacing alcohol abuse as an addiction, with an accompanying neglect of family responsibilities caused by gambling addiction; a decrease in family and other community social activities as they are replaced by casino gambling as the dominant social activity; problems with child care as gamblers and casino workers alike are relying on young people to provide child care, or neglecting to provide child care altogether because extended family members are either working in casinos or gambling.

There was a deep sense from most of the informants that the presence of casino gaming was having yet undetermined effects on traditional tribal culture (values, beliefs, ways of being), that these effects were most probably negative and would become apparent in the near future. Informants spoke of a decline in leveling (a sharing of material possessions based upon traditional values) with the increase in jobs, money, and the rise in individual materialism.

So it appears that while there are benefits, gaming has exacerbated our uncertainties about the future. How will our traditional culture be affected? What are the social costs? Will Congress or the state legislatures try to limit the growth of casinos or put unnecessary, burdensome regulations on gaming operations to the point of making them unprofitable? Will states open their own casino operations, undermining or creating undue competition for rural casino operations? When will we see the oft-talked-about downturn in the economic cycle of gambling? So the future, while certainly much brighter than when I was growing up in the 1950s, remains clouded.

BANGISHIMOG
(sunset)

The Ojibwe people will always be here because we are part of a much larger story of our own weaving, a story foretold by our ancestors and lived by all those who travel on the good road.

Summary

I BEGAN THIS CHAPTER by describing how my family survived during the 1950s, a time of welfare dependency and grinding poverty, of selling pulp wood, catfish, rabbits, weasel skins, wild rice, and blue-berries and of picking potatoes in order to live. Most of us made it through those times. Through the years, however, there were some — my grandparents and parents, two brothers, a sister, and my only daughter — who fell along the way. Now, as I stand on the pinnacle of the third hill of my life, I am reminded of my responsibility to give back and to live the vision prescribed for me when I was a young child: to put our story into words, to teach. And far off in the distance towers yet another hill.

We are a people as old as stone. And we will be here forever, long after the last lawsuit to challenge our sovereignty, long after the last HUD house has fallen back into the earth, long after the last casino has been converted to a community center. Our great-grandchildren, as well as their children, will still be Anishinabeg. And although we of the present generation will have traveled to the spirit world, the Ojibwe of future generations will still seek our advice, as we have done with our ancestors. We will be here because we are part of a much larger story of our own weaving, a story foretold by our ancestors and lived by all those who travel on the good road (Bibeau, 1971, p. 14):

We will endure because we are Indian. And being Indian is not simply living in the forest, or mountains or plains, or skin, features, or beads, or sense of history, or language or song: it is living in peace within the great cycles of nature which the Great Spirit has bestowed upon his children, and it is living within the tribal fold. What some others may call "community." And it is good! It is good to live within the Tribe on this reservation in these lands of our fathers. And so it has been from the most ancient of times.

Opposite page: DA-AABIJI-MINOGANAWAABAMIGONAAN
(Hopefully we will always be well watched over)

Bibliography

OJIBWEMOWIN, Ojibwe Oral Tradition

Clifford, J. (1986). "On Ethnographic Allegory." In J. Clifford and G.E. Marcus, eds., *Writing Culture: The Poetics and Politics of Ethnography* (pp. 98-121). Berkeley: University of California Press.

Copyway, G. (1987). "The Traditional History and Characteristic Sketches of the Ojibway Nation." In G. Vizenor, *Touchwood* (pp. 59-89). St. Paul: New Rivers Press.

Christensen, R. A., Ruhnke, W., and Shannon, T. (1995). Ojibwe Language Institute: *Elders Speak*. Unpublished proposal.

Crawford, J. (1996). "Seven Hypotheses on Language Loss Causes and Cures." In G. Cantoni, ed., *Stabilizing Indigenous Languages* (pp. 186-198). Flagstaff: Northern Arizona University.

Denny, J. P. (1991). "Rational Thought in Oral Culture and Literate Decontextualization." In D. Olson and N. Torrance, eds., *Literacy and Orality* (pp. 90-101). London: Cambridge University Press.

Donaldson, M. (1979). *Children's Minds*. New York: Norton.

Feldman, C. Fleisher. (1991). "Oral Metalanguage." In D. Olson and N. Torrance, eds., *Literacy and Orality* (pp. 45-65). London: Cambridge University Press.

Grover, L. (1999). *The Effects of Boarding School on Those Who Attended and Their Children*. University of Minnesota. Unpublished doctoral thesis.

Johnston, B. (1976). *Ojibwe Heritage*. Lincoln: University of Nebraska Press.

McCutchen, D. (1989). *The Red Record*. Garden City, New York: Avery Publishing Group.

Peacock, T., ed. (1998). *A Forever Story: The People and Community of the Fond du Lac Reservation*. Cloquet, Minnesota: Fond du Lac Band of Lake Superior Chippewa.

Scribner, S. and Cole, M. (1981). *The Psychology of Literacy*. Cambridge: Harvard University Press.

Vizenor, G. (1965). *Anishinabe Nagamon*. Minneapolis: Nodin Press.

Vizenor, G. (1984). *The People Named the Chippewa*. Minneapolis: University of Minnesota Press.

GAKINA-AWIIYA, We Are All Related

Axtell, H. & Aragon, M. (1997). *A Little Bit of Wisdom*. Lewiston, Idaho: Confluence Press.

Bruchac, J., ed. (1983). *Songs From This Earth On Turtle's Back*. Greenfield Center, New York: Greenfield Review Press.

Clifton, J. (1987). *Wisconsin Death March: Explaining the Extremes of Old Northwest Indian Removal*. Transactions of the Wisconsin Academy of Sciences, Arts and Letters, 75: 1-39.

Cudato, M. & Bruchac, J. (1991). *Keepers of the Animals*. Golden, Colorado: Fulcrum Publishing.

Kohl, J. (1985). *Kitchi-Gami: Life among the Lake Superior Ojibway*. St. Paul: Minnesota Historical Society Press.

Neihardt, J. (1932). *Black Elk Speaks*. Lincoln: University of Nebraska Press.

Ojibwe Curriculum Committee. (1973). *The Land of the Ojibwe*. St. Paul: Minnesota Historical Society Press.

Peacock, T., ed. (1998). *A Forever Story: The People and Community of the Fond du Lac Reservation*. Cloquet, Minnesota: Fond du Lac Band of Lake Superior Chippewa.

Ray, A. (1974). *Indians in the Fur Trade: Their Role as Trappers, Hunters, and Middlemen in the Lands Southwest of Hudson Bay*. Toronto: University of Toronto Press.

Warren, W. (1984). *History of the Ojibway People*. St. Paul: Minnesota Historical Society Press.

Zinn, H. (1980). *A People's History of the United States*. New York: HarperCollins Publishers.

GIKINOO'AMAADIWIN, We Gain Knowledge

Beaulieu, D. (1998). Personal interview.

Broker, I. (1983). *Night Flying Woman*. St. Paul: Minnesota Historical Society Press.

Cleary, L. Miller, & Peacock, T. (1998). *Collected Wisdom: American Indian Education*. Needham Heights, Massachusetts: Allyn and Bacon.

Duluth Indian Education Committee. (1976). *A Long Time Ago Is Just Like Today*. Duluth, Minnesota: Duluth Public Schools.

Gilliland, H. (1988). *Teaching the Native American*. Dubuque, Iowa: Kendall-Hunt.

Grover, L. (1999). *The Effects of Boarding School on Those Who Attended and Their Children*. University of Minnesota. Unpublished doctoral thesis.

Hilger, I. (1992). *Chippewa Child Life and Its Cultural Background*. St. Paul: Minnesota Historical Society Press.

Johnston, B. (1976). *Ojibway Heritage*. Lincoln: University of Nebraska Press.

Johnston, B. (1982). *Ojibway Ceremonies*. Lincoln: University of Nebraska Press.

Peacock, T., ed. (1998). *A Forever Story: The People and Community of the Fond du Lac Reservation*. Cloquet,

Minnesota: Fond du Lac Band of Lake Superior Chippewa.

Quality Education for Minorities Project. (1990). *Education that Works: An Action Plan for the Education of Minorities.* Cambridge: Massachusetts Institute of Technology.

Reyhner, J. & Eder, J. (1992). *A History of Indian Education.* In Jon Reyhner, ed., *Teaching the American Indian students.* Norman: University of Oklahoma Press.

Rogers, J. (1973). *Red World and White.* Norman: University of Oklahoma Press.

Vizenor, G. (1987). *Touchwood.* St. Paul: New Rivers Press.

Warren, W. (1984). *History of the Ojibway People.* St. Paul: Minnesota Historical Society Press.

Zinn, H. (1980). *A People's History of the United States.* New York: Harper Collins Publishers.

BIMAADIZIWIN, A Healthy Way of Life

Big Eagle, D. (1983). "My Grandfather Was a Quantum Physicist". In Joseph Bruchac, ed., *Songs From This Earth On Turtle's Back.* Greenfield, Connecticut: Greenfield Review Press.

Broker, I. (1983). *Night Flying Woman.* St. Paul: Minnesota Historical Society Press.

Cleary, L., and Peacock, T. (1998). *Collected Wisdom: American Indian Education.* Needham Heights, Massachusetts: Allyn and Bacon.

Hilger, I. (1992). *Chippewa Child Life.* St. Paul: Minnesota Historical Society Press.

Johnston, B. (1976). *Ojibway Heritage.* Lincoln: University of Nebraska Press.

Moore, S., and Brenning, R. (1997). *Walking Upstream.* Duluth: Crescent and Quill Press.

Peacock, T., ed. (1998). *A Forever Story: The People and Community of the Fond du Lac Reservation.* Cloquet, Minnesota: Fond du Lac Band of Lake Superior Chippewa.

Weatherford, J. (1988). *Indian Givers.* New York: Ballantine Books.

GWAYAKOCHIGEWIN, Doing Things the Right Way

Christenson, R. (1999). *Anishinabeg Medicine Wheel Leadership: The Work of David F. Courchene, Jr.* Unpublished doctoral dissertation, University of Minnesota.

Deloria, V. (1969). *Custer Died for Your Sins.* New York: Macmillan Company.

Deloria, V., and Lytle, C. (1984). *The Nations Within: The Past and Future of American Indian Sovereignty.* New York: Pantheon Books.

Ebbott, Elizabeth, ed. (1985). *Indians in Minnesota.* Minneapolis: University of Minnesota Press for the League of Women Voters of Minnesota.

Jaakola, L. (1999). *Leadership and Governance.* Unpublished paper.

Johnston, B. (1976). *Ojibwe Heritage.* Lincoln: University of Nebraska Press.

Johnston, B. (1979). *Ojibwe Ceremonies.* Lincoln: University of Nebraska Press.

Ojibwe Curriculum Committee. (1973). *The Land of the Ojibwe.* St. Paul: Minnesota Historical Society.

Peacock, T. (1988). *Internal Tribal Disputes in the Age of Self-determination.* Unpublished doctoral dissertation, Harvard Graduate School of Education.

Warren, W. (1984). *History of the Ojibway People.* St. Paul: Minnesota Historical Society Press.

Wax, M. (1971). *Indian Americans.* Englewood Cliffs, New Jersey: Prentice-Hall.

Weatherford, J. (1988). *Indian Givers.* New York: Ballantine Books.

Williamson, W. (1832). *History of Maine.* Hallowell, Maine: Masters and Company.

GAA-MIINIGOOYANG, That Which is Given To Us

Bibeau, D. (1971). *We Will Endure.* Events. June. pp. 13-14.

Cleary, L. & Peacock, T. (1998). *Collected Wisdom: American Indian Education*: Needham Heights, Massachusetts: Allyn and Bacon.

Jaakola, L. (1999). *Survival and Economic Development.* Unpublished paper.

McCutchen, D. (1993). *The Red Record.* Garden City Park, New York: Avery Publishing Group.

Ojibwe Curriculum Committee. (1973). *The Land of the Ojibwe.* St. Paul: Minnesota Historical Society.

Peacock, T., ed. (1998). *A Forever Story: The People and Community of the Fond du Lac Reservation.* Cloquet, Minnesota: Fond du Lac Band of Lake Superior Chippewa.

Peacock, T., Day, P., & Peacock, R. (1998). *At What Cost? The Social Impact of American Indian Gaming.* Journal of Health and Social Policy 10, 4. pp. 23-34.

Ray, A. (1974). *Indians in the Fur Trade: Their Role as Trappers, Hunters, and Middlemen in the Lands Southwest of Hudson Bay.* Toronto: University of Toronto Press.

Warren, W. (1984). *History of the Ojibway People.* St. Paul: Minnesota Historical Society Press.

Illustration Credits

Cover: *Circle of Life*, by Ojibwe artist Joe Geschick
ii. *Sunrise over Lake Superior*, photo by Marlene Wisuri
14–15. *Story Teller*, acrylic on wood by Carl Gawboy
16. *Turtle Image*, watercolor by Jeff Chapman, Courtesy of Min-no-aya-win Clinic
17. *Spirit Tree*, Minnesota Office of Tourism
18. *Eagle*, photo by Dudley Edmondson, Raptor Works
19. *Rushing Water in Spring*, photo by Marlene Wisuri
20. *Flood with Rainbow*, photo by Marlene Wisuri
21. *Moosoog*, photo by Dudley Edmondson, Raptor Works
22t. *Muskrat*, photo by Dudley Edmondson, Raptor Works
22b. *Map of migrations and locations*, Tim Roufs
23. *Mackinac Island*, from Castlenau, *Vues et Souvenir du Nord*, pl. 26, The Newberry Library
24t. *Fur Trade at Grand Portage*, watercolor by Carl Gawboy
24b. *Sault Ste. Marie at the Rapids*, Sault Ste. Marie Tribe of Chippewa Indians
25. *Village at Sault Ste. Marie*, Benjamin Franklin Childs, Minnesota Historical Society
26. *La Pointe, or Madeline Island*, State Historical Society of Wisconsin, sketch by Aindi-bi-tunk
27. *Bear Feast*, Milwaukee Public Museum
28. *Nick Hocking at Fond du Lac Tribal and Community College*, photo by Jeff Thompson, Cloquet Pine Knot
29t. *Winter Ice*, photo by Marlene Wisuri
29b. *Men's Fish Dance*, Lac du Flambeau
30. *Child Learning Language*, Charles Curtis, *Duluth News Tribune*
31. *Woman Parching Rice at Nett Lake*, 1946, Monroe P. Killy, Minnesota Historical Society
32. *Father Baraga*, photo by Marlene Wisuri
33. *Early School in Grand Portage*, George A. Newton, St. Louis County Historical Society
34. *Pictographs*, photo by Sarah Kransur
35. *Woman with Blueberries*, watercolor by Patrick DesJarlait, Minnesota Historical Society
36t. *Churinga*, bronze, George Morrison, photo by Marlene Wisuri
36b. *George Morrison*, photo by Marlene Wisuri
37. *Man in Traditional Dance Outfit*, photo by Marlene Wisuri
38–39. *Indian Cemetery at Wisconsin Point*, Carlton County Historical Society
40. *Pines at Wisconsin Point*, photo by Marlene Wisuri
41. *Gravestone in St. Francis Cemetery, Superior, Wisconsin*, photo by Marlene Wisuri
42t. *White Rose*, photo by Marlene Wisuri
42b. *Deer*, photo by Dudley Edmondson, Raptor Works
43. *Ravens*, photo by Dudley Edmondson, Raptor Works
44. *Scenic Overview*, photo by Marlene Wisuri
45. *Bear image painted on a rock* by Julie Bellager near Little Sand Bay, Wisconsin
46. *Beaver Hooked Rug*, Grand Portage Monument
47. *American Fur Trading Post at Fond du Lac*, from *Tour to the Lakes*, Thomas L. McKenney, 1827, postcard issued by the St. Louis County Historical Society
48. *Hunter in the Snow with Gun*, 1870, Charles A. Zimmerman, Minnesota Historical Society
49t. *Treaty Diagram*, from a drawing by Seth Eastman of a birch-bark pictograph, reproduced in *Historical and Statistical Information Respecting the History, Condition, and Prospects of the Indian Tribes of the United States*, Henry Rowe Schoolcraft, Volume I, 1851, Duluth Public Library
49b. *Beaver*, painting by Noel DuCharme from the collection of Wendy Savage
50. *Women and Children Guarding Corn Field*, photo by Adrian J. Ebell, Minnesota Historical Society
51. *Treaty map of ceded territory*, Great Lakes Indian Fish and Wildlife Commission
52. *Buffalo on Prairie*, photo by Dudley Edmondson, Raptor Works
53. *Louis Riel burial site, St. Boniface, Manitoba*, photo by Marlene Wisuri
54. *Chief Bugonaygeshig*, Cass County Historical Society
55t. *Annuity Payment*, Charles Zimmerman, Minnesota Historical Society
55b. *Leech Lake Delegation in Washington*, 1899, DeLancey Gill, Minnesota Historical Society
56. *Swan River Logging Camp*, Minnesota Historical Society
57. *Assimilation Dress*, photo by Allen Beaulieu, Courtesy of the Ojibwe Art Expo, Laura Heit, artist
58. *American Indian Movement*, Dick Bancroft, Chippewa Valley Museum
59. *Mining Demonstration*, Great Lakes Indian Fish and Wildlife Commission
60. *Sovereignty is NOT for Sale*, Great Lakes Indian Fish and Wildlife Commission
61t. *Treaty decision Headline*, *Masinaigan*
61b. *March on Michigan capitol*, 1995, Win Awenen Nisitotung, Sault Ste. Marie Tribe of Chippewa Indians
62. *Walt Bresette's staff* photo by Kathy Olson
63. *Cobweb*, photo by Marlene Wisuri
64. *Woman with Child*, State Historical Society of Wisconsin
66. *Headstart at Fond du Lac*, photo by Marlene Wisuri
67. *National Archives*
68. *Children in Wild Rice Camp*, Minnesota Historical Society
69. *Women and Girls near Grand Marais*, Minnesota Historical Society
70. *Boy's Mocassin Game*, Monroe P. Killy, Minnesota Historical Society
71. *Men's Moccasin Game*, Robert G. Beaulieu, Minnesota Historical Society
72. *Visioning*, photo by Jeff Thompson
74. *Ojibwe Family at Cass Lake*, Minnesota Historical Society
75. *Clan symbols*, *The Aborigines of Minnesota*, 1911, Minnesota Historical Society
76. *Young Man and Woman*, photo by Charles H. Zimmerman, Minnesota Historical Society
77. *Boarding School at St. Benedict's Mission on White Earth Reservation*, Minnesota Historical Society
78. *Classes at Ojibwe School*, Lac du Flambeau
79. *Lac du Flambeau Band*, collection of Elaine Kraska
80. *Odana Cemetery*, photo by Marlene Wisuri
81. *Boarding School*, Clark Historical Library
82t. *St. Mary's School*, Minnesota Historical Society
82b. *Ponemah Indian School*, Minnesota Historical Society
83. *Students at Mille Lacs Vineland*, Minnesota Historical Society
84. *Farming at St. Mary's*, Minnesota Historical Society
85. *Ojibwe Girl at Cass Lake Library*, Minnesota Historical Society
86t. *David Beaulieu*, WDSE Public Television
86b. *Michigan Education Protest*, Sault Ste. Marie Tribe of Chippewa Indians
87. *Girl with Computer*, Kathy Strauss,

Duluth News Tribune
89. *Grandmother with Child Sugaring*, WDSE Public Television
90–91. *Swamp Tea*, photo by Marlene Wisuri
93. *Midwife from Sugar Island*, Bayliss Public Library, Sault Ste. Marie
94. *Painted Turtle*, photo by Dudley Edmondson, Raptor Works
95. *Medicine Man's Home and Teepee at Grand Portage*, Minnesota Historical Society
96. *Elizabeth Pine*, Bayliss Public Library, Sault Ste. Marie
97. Epidemic map, detail, Newberry Library from *The Atlas of Great Lakes Indian History*, University of Oklahoma Press, 1987
98. *Spirit Pole*, photo by Monroe P. Killy, Minnesota Historical Society
99t. *Hospital at White Earth*, Minnesota Historical Society
99b. *Hospital Workers*, Dan Anderson collection
100. *Child Receiving Medicine*, Minnesota Historical Society
101. *Indian Health Service Clinic*, Minnesota Historical Society
102t. *Hospital at Pipestone School*, Minnesota Historical Society
102b. *Health Camp*, Minnesota Historical Society
103. *Jack in the Pulpit*, photo by Marlene Wisuri
104t. *Trillium*, photo by Marlene Wisuri
104b. *Golden Rod*, photo by Marlene Wisuri
105. *Mash-ka-wisen Treatment Center*, Bob King, Duluth News Tribune
106. *Jimmy Jackson*, photo by Betsy Albert
107. *Sobriety Pow-wow*, photo by Marlene Wisuri
108. *Kathy Smart*, Chippewa Valley Museum
109. *Dr. Arne Vainio*, photo by Rocky Wilkinson, Fond du Lac
110. *Cass Lake Hospital*, WDSE Public Television
111. *Birch Trees in Summer*, photo by Marlene Wisuri
112–113. *Smoking in Council*, Minnesota Historical Society
114t. *Singba W'Ossin*, from *The Indian Tribes of North America*, McKenney & Hall, 1933, Duluth Public Library
114b. *Chief Buffalo*, State Historical Society of Wisconsin
115t. *Bug-o-nay-ge-shig*, Minnesota Historical Society
115b. *Flat Mouth*, from *The Aborigines of Minnesota*, 1911, Minnesota Historical Society
116. *Crane*, photo by Dudley Edmondson, Raptor Works
117. *Loonsfoot*, Carlton County Historical Society
118. *Chief Shoppenagon with Wife and Daughter*, Marquette Mission Park and Museum of Ojibwa Culture, St. Ignace, MI
119. *Chief White Cloud*, Minnesota Historical Society
120. *Maji Ga Bow*, Carlton County Historical Society
121. *Chiefs at Lake of the Woods, 1922*, Carl Gustaf Linde, Minnesota Historical Society
122. *Peter Graves*, photo by Arch Grahn, Minnesota Historical Society
123. *Tribal Court Building/Baraga*, photo by Marlene Wisuri
124. Map of current reservations, WDSE Public Television
126t. *Gaiashkibos with Billboard*, Great Lakes Indian Fish and Wildlife Commission
126b. *Veterans' Memorial*, photo by Marlene Wisuri
127. *Tom Shingobe*, photo by Randy Croce, Minnesota Historical Society
129t. *Walt Bresette*, photo by Kathy Olson
129b. *Winona LaDuke*, photo by Keri Pickett

130. *People Outside Cabin*, photo by George Niles Ryan, Minnesota Historical Society
131. *Gus Lemieux*, photo by Jeff Thompson, Cloquet Pine Knot
132–133. *Canoe Building*, photo by Truman W. Ingersoll, Minnesota Historical Society
134. *Children Selling Blueberries*, photo by Carl Gustaf Linde, Minnesota Historical Society
135. *Moose Hunt at Grand Portage*, photo by Marlene Wisuri
136. *Selling Maple Sugar*, Minnesota Historical Society
137. *Wild Ricing*, photo by Ritzenthaler, Milwaukee Public Museum
138. *Muskrat Trapper*, Milwaukee Public Museum
139. *Woman Feeding Chickens*, Minnesota Historical Society
140. *Mining Pits*, photo by Marlene Wisuri
141. *Jerking Venison*, Milwaukee Public Museum
142. *Muskie Spearing*, Milwaukee Public Museum
143. *Rossel William*, Lac du Flambeau
144. *Woman with Crafs*, photo by A.J. Kingsbury, Lac du Flambeau
145. *Boat Building*, Minnesota Historical Society
146. *Wild Rice*, Minnesota Historical Society
147. *Receiving Government Checks*, Minnesota Historical Society
148. *Woman in Sugar Camp*, Randy Croce, Minnesota Historical Society
149–150. *Soaring Eagle Casino and Resort in Saginaw, Michigan*, Bathazar Korab/Saginaw Chippewa Indian Tribe
151. *Sunset*, photo by Jeff Thompson
152. *Couple on Shore at Mashkawisen Pow-wow*, photo by Marlene Wisuri
153. *Moonrise*, photo by Marlene Wisuri
158. *Charlie Wayashe*, Sault Ste. Marie Tribe of Chippewa Indians

About the Television Series

THIS BOOK WAS CONCEIVED as a companion to the public television series *Waasa Inaabidaa—We Look in all Directions* by award-winning producer Lorraine Norrgard (*A Gift to One, A Gift to Many: James Jackson Sr., Looks Into the Night*). Created in answer to numerous requests for more information about the Anishinaabe/Ojibwe, this six-part series is the most comprehensive programming about the tribe ever created for television. It represents the contributions of nineteen Ojibwe communities (that form the second-largest tribe in North America) and more than two hundred Ojibwe individuals.

Spanning five hundred years of change and endurance, the story of the Anishinaabe/Ojibwe people is a compelling one of adaptation and survival, desperation and ingenuity, bitter betrayals and stunning victories. Though rooted in the Great Lakes region, this story has much in common with other indigenous nations throughout the United States and Canada and provides valuable lessons for all people.

Narrated by Winona LaDuke, Ojibwe, each hour-long episode explores Ojibwe culture from pre-contact times to the present, focusing on topics of language, leadership, economic development, education, health, and the Ojibwe relationship to the environment. Written by James Fortier, Ojibwe, this illuminating series combines interviews with historians and Ojibwe elders, leaders, and youth with thousands of archival photographs, artwork, animation, and dramatic scenes to illustrate the traditional four seasons' life cycle of the Ojibwe people. The original soundtrack by noted composer Peter Buffet (*Dances With Wolves, 500 Nations*) features performances by more than a dozen Objiwe singers, drummers, and musicians.

A comprehensive teacher's guide for each episode is available through the program's educational website: www.ojibwe.org. Copies of the television programs and the soundtrack can ordered from WDSE-TV, PBS-Eight (Duluth, Minnesota) by phone (218) 724-8567, or at www.wdse.org.

Charlie Wayashe, Sault Ste. Marie Tribe of Chippewa Indians

The production staff is grateful and honored to have been able to bring this profound story to light. It is their hope that this gift of knowledge will mean as much to future generations as it has to its makers.

Designed by
Barbara J. Arney
Stillwater, MN

Typefaces are
Gill Sans
Galahad
Bembo